# PRIESTHOOD in the THIRD MILLENNIUM

# PRIESTHOOD
# in the THIRD
# MILLENNIUM

*Addresses of Pope John Paul II*
*1993*

Compiled by
Rev. James P. Socias

**Scepter Publishers**
Princeton, New Jersey

**Midwest Theological Forum**
Chicago

This edition of *Priesthood in the Third Millennium* is published by:

**Scepter Publishers**
20 Nassau St.
Princeton, NJ 08542

and

**Midwest Theological Forum**
1410 W. Lexington St.
Chicago, IL 60607

The **Midwest Theological Forum** is an educational service organized by priests of the Prelature of Opus Dei and other diocesan priests.

Reprinted with permission from Libreria Editrice Vaticana

*Printed in the United States of America*

ISBN 0-933932-71-5

# Contents

# FOREWORD

I am writing this foreword on March 31, 1994, Holy Thursday, the feast of the ministerial priesthood, the day of the Chrism Mass and the Mass of the Lord's Supper. On this day Pope John Paul II has once again made us, his "dear Brothers in the Priesthood," the gift of a letter, the sixteenth in a series. He invites us to reflect on the Eucharist and the Priesthood, entrusts to us his "Letter to Families," and encourages us to "fidelity to our vocation" which "builds up the Church."

Exactly a year ago, on Wednesday, March 31, 1993 the Holy Father began his catechesis during his General Audiences on the theme of the *presbyterate*; he concluded it on Wednesday, September 29, 1993: eighteen talks in all. They form the principal part of the present volume.

This catechesis on the priesthood is part of a larger series dedicated to the *Church*, begun on July 10, 1991. Pope John Paul II addressed the origin, nature, and mission of the Church. Then he continued on to the ministry of bishops and the Successor of Peter; ministerial priesthood, and the diaconate. No doubt, when reflecting upon the Church we find ourselves immersed in the splendor of so many truths— of course, also those regarding the laity, about which the Pope is presently speaking in his weekly catechesis. Nor does he forget the persons who have a special consecration: they are mentioned, for instance, in two discourses published in this book (cf. pp. 127 and 148), and for them a General Assembly of the Synod of Bishops will be celebrated in October 1994.

It is then in such a broader context of a deep and clear analysis of the Church and its components, that the Holy Father's catechesis on the presbyterate has its place, and necessarily so. Hence the opportunity of enjoying the fullness and beauty of our faith in the one, holy, catholic, and apostolic Church.

Pope John Paul II has of course devoted his magisterial solicitude to the priesthood on innumerable occasions during the sixteen years of his pontificate, always with the intention of fraternal love and solidarity. This work includes three other discourses (pp. 131ff.). One cannot but recall also the post-synodal apostolic exhortation "Pastores Dabo Vobis" of March 25, 1992.

The eighteen talks of the Holy Father's Wednesday catechesis deserve special attention, because of their organic unity and exhaustiveness. The idea of presenting them in this volume is no doubt extremely opportune and useful. Here we find the most profound dimension of our being and the unfolding of our mission as priests. Our life and our ministry receive light and strength from these words. This book can truly be called a 'priestly manual' of exceptional merit to be read and to be meditated upon in a prayerful spirit.

With their unique value as an expression of the magisterium of the Successor of Peter, these speeches offer a content of high quality and importance from doctrinal, spiritual and pastoral points of view. Such indeed is their relevance, that they are quoted among the sources and references of the "Directory for Priestly Ministry and Life" which was released by the Congregation for Clergy with today's date, Holy Thursday 1994.

This publication is a praiseworthy initiative of "Midwest Theological Forum" founded by priests of the Prelature of Opus Dei and other diocesan priests. They are interested in advancing theological study, and surely a book of this kind promotes authentic, sound and solid doctrine. May many benefit from it.

The title given is "Priesthood in the Third Millennium," and rightly so, as the Church is now preparing for the great Jubilee of the Year 2000. The presbyterate is an essential element as we look toward the next millennium. The truth about the ministerial priesthood, which the Holy Father presents to us in all its splendor, will continue to be valid for all generations to come, just as Jesus Christ, Our Lord, who is "the same yesterday, today and forever" (Heb. 13:8).

Holy Thursday, March 31, 1994

Archbishop Agostino Cacciavillan

Apostolic Nuncio

# I

# Priests: Sharers in the Priesthood of Christ

General Audience of Wednesday March 31,1993

*In the sacrament of Holy Orders priests receive a share in the pastoral authority by which Christ builds up, sanctifies and rules his Church.*

1. Today we are beginning a new series of catecheses dedicated to the *presbyterate* and to *presbyters,* who, as we know, are the closest coworkers of the bishops in whose consecration and priestly mission they share. I will talk about this by adhering strictly to the New Testament texts and by following the approach of the Second Vatican Council, which has been the style of these catecheses.

I begin my development of this theme with deep affection for these close coworkers of the episcopal order, to whom I feel close and whom I love in the Lord, as I have said since the beginning of my Pontificate, particularly in my first Letter to Priests of the whole world, written for Holy Thursday, 1979.

2. It must immediately be pointed out that the priesthood, in every degree, and thus in both bishops and presbyters, is a participation in the priesthood of Christ, who, according to the Letter to the Hebrews, is the one "High Priest" of the new and eternal covenant, who "offered himself once for

all" in a sacrifice of infinite value that remains unchangeable and unceasing at the very heart of the economy of salvation.[1]

There is no further need or possibility of other priests in addition to or alongside the one Mediator, Christ,[2] the point of union and reconciliation between mankind and God,[3] the Word made flesh, full of grace,[4] the true and definitive *hiereús,* or Priest,[5] who on earth "took away sin by his sacrifice"[6] and in heaven continues to make intercession for his faithful,[7] until they attain the heavenly inheritance won and promised by him. No one else in the new covenant is *hiereús* in the same sense.

### Sharers in the Apostles' Mission

3. The participation in Christ's one priesthood, which is exercised in several degrees, was instituted by Christ, who wanted differentiated functions in his Church as in a well-organized social body, and for the function of leadership he established ministers of his priesthood.[8] He conferred on them the sacrament of Orders to constitute them officially as priests who would work in his name and with his power by offering sacrifice and forgiving sins.

The Council notes: "Thus Christ sent the Apostles as he himself had been sent by the Father, and then through the Apostles made successors, the bishops, sharers in his consecration and mission. The function of the bishops' ministry was handed over in a subordinate degree to presbyters so that they might be appointed in the order of the presbyterate and be coworkers of the episcopal order for the proper fulfillment of the apostolic mission that had been entrusted to it by Christ."[9]

This will of Christ clearly appears in the Gospel, from which we know that Jesus assigned to Peter and the Twelve a supreme authority in his Church, but he also wanted coworkers for their mission. What the evangelist Luke attests is significant, namely, that after Jesus sent the Twelve on mission,[10] he sent a still larger number of disciples, to indicate as it were that the mission of the Twelve was not enough for the work of evangelization. "After this the Lord appointed 72 others whom he sent ahead of him in pairs to every town and place he intended to visit."[11]

Doubtless this step only prefigures the ministry that Christ will formally institute later on. However, it already shows the divine Master's intention to introduce a sizable number of coworkers into the "vineyard." Jesus chose the Twelve from among a larger group of disciples.[12] These "disciples", in the sense of the term used in the Gospel texts, are not only those who believe in Jesus but those who follow him and want to accept his teaching as the Master and devote themselves to his work. And Jesus involves them in his mission. According to Luke, it was precisely on this occasion that Jesus said the words: "The harvest is abundant but the laborers are few."[13]

Thus he indicated that, in his mind, relative to the experience of the first ministry, the number of workers was too small. That was true not only then, but for all times—including our own—when the problem has become particularly acute. We have to deal with it, feeling spurred on and at the same time comforted by these words and—so to speak—by Jesus' gaze on the fields where laborers are needed for harvesting the grain. Jesus gave the example by his initiative, which could be called "vocations" promotion: he sent 72 disciples in addition to the 12 Apostles.

4. According to the Gospel, Jesus assigned to the 72 disciples a mission *like* that of the Twelve: the disciples were sent to proclaim the coming of God's kingdom. They will carry out this preaching in the name of Christ and with his authority: "Whoever listens to you listens to me. Whoever rejects you rejects me. And whoever rejects me rejects the one who sent me."[14]

### Distinct from Bishops

Like the Twelve,[15] the disciples receive the power to expel evil spirits, so much so that after their first experiences they say to Jesus: "Lord, even the demons are subject to us because of your name." This power is confirmed by Jesus himself: "I have observed Satan fall like lightning from the sky. Behold I have given you the power 'to tread upon serpents' and upon the full force of the enemy. . . ."[16]

This also means that they participate with the Twelve in the *redemptive work* of the one Priest of the new covenant, Christ, who wanted to confer on them too a mission and powers like those of the Twelve. The establishment of the presbyterate, therefore, does not only answer one of the practical necessities of the bishops, who feel the need for coworkers, but derives from an explicit intention of Christ.

5. In fact, we already find that in the early Christian era presbyters *(presbýteroi)* are present and functioning in the Church of the Apostles and of the first bishops, their successors.[17] In these New Testament books it is not always easy to distinguish between "presbyters" and "bishops" regarding the duties assigned to them; but very early on, already in the Church of the Apostles, the two categories of those sharing in Christ's mission and priesthood appear to take shape.

They are found again later and more clearly described in the works of the subapostolic writers,[18] until in the common terminology of the Church in Jerusalem, Rome and the other communities of the East and West, the word *bishop is* finally reserved for the one head and pastor of the community, while the term *presbyter* designates a minister who works in dependence on a bishop.

6. Following Christian tradition and in conformity with Christ's will as attested in the New Testament, the Second Vatican Council speaks of presbyters as ministers who do not have "the supreme degree of the priesthood" and who, in exercising their power, depend on bishops. On the other

hand, they are associated with them "by reason of their priestly dignity."[19] This association is rooted in the sacrament of Orders: "Because it is joined with the episcopal order, the office of presbyters shares in the authority by which Christ himself builds up, sanctifies and rules his Body."[20] Presbyters too bear "the image of Christ, the supreme and eternal Priest."[21] Therefore they participate in Christ's pastoral authority: this is the characteristic note of their ministry, based on the sacrament of Orders conferred on them.

We read in the Decree *Presbyterorum Ordinis:* "Hence the priesthood of presbyters, while presupposing the sacraments of initiation, is nevertheless conferred by its own particular sacrament. Through that sacrament presbyters, by the anointing of the Holy Spirit, are signed with a special character and so are configured to Christ the Priest in such a way that they are able to act in the person of Christ the Head."[22]

**Recipients of Special Graces**

This character, in those who receive it through the sacramental anointing of the Holy Spirit, is a sign of: *a special consecration,* in relationship to Baptism and Confirmation; *a deeper configuration to Christ the Priest,* who makes them his active ministers in the official worship of God and in sanctifying their brothers and sisters, the *ministerial powers* to be exercised in the name of Christ, the Head and Shepherd of the Church.[23]

7. In the presbyter's soul the character is also a sign and vehicle of the special graces for carrying out the ministry, graces related to the sanctifying grace that Holy Orders imparts as a sacrament both at the time it is conferred and throughout his exercise of and growth in the ministry. It thus surrounds and involves the presbyter in an economy of sanctification, which the ministry itself implies both for the one who exercises it and for those who benefit from it

in the various sacraments and other activities performed by their pastors.

The whole Church garners the fruit of the sanctification resulting from the ministry of presbyter-pastors: both diocesan priests and those who, having received Holy Orders under any title or in any form, carry out their activity in communion with the diocesan bishops and the Successor of Peter.

8. The profound ontology of the consecration received in Orders and the dynamism of sanctification that it entails in the ministry certainly exclude any secularized interpretation of the priestly ministry, as if the presbyter were simply dedicated to establishing justice or spreading love in the world.

The presbyter participates ontologically in the priesthood of Christ; he is truly consecrated, a "man of the sacred", designated like Christ to the worship that ascends to the Father and to the evangelizing mission by which he spreads and distributes sacred realities-the truth, the grace of God— to his brothers and sisters. This is the priest's true identity; this is the essential requirement of the priestly ministry in today's world too.

## NOTES

1. Cf. Heb 7:24-28
2. Cf. Heb 9:15, Rom 5:15-19; I Tm 2:5
3. Cf. 2 Cor 5:14-20
4. Cf. Jn 1:1 - 18
5. Heb 5:6; 10:21
6. Heb 9:26
7. Cf. Heb 7:25
8. Cf. *Catechism of the Catholic Church* [= CCC], n. 1554
9. *Presbyterorum ordinis*, n. 2; CCC, n. 1562
10. Cf. 9:1-6
11. Lk 10:1

12. Cf. Lk 6:12, 13
13. Lk 10:2
14. Lk 10:16
15. Cf. Mk 6:7; Lk 9:1
16. Lk 10:17-19
17. Cf. Acts 11:30; 14:23; 15:2, 4, 6, 22, 23, 41; 16:4; 20:17; 21:18; I Tm 4:14; 5:17, 19; Ti 1:5; Jas 5:14; 1 Pt 5:1, 5, 15; 2 Jn 1; 3 Jn 1
18. Like Pope St. Clement's *Letter to the Corinthians,* the *Letters* of St. Ignatius of Antioch, the *Shepherd of Hermas,* etc.
19. *Lumen gentium,* n. 28; cf. CCC, n. 1564
20. *Presbyterorum ordinis,* n. 2; cf. CCC, n. 1563
21. *Lumen gentium,* n. 28
22. *Presbyterorum ordinis,* n. 2; CCC, n. 1563
23. Cf. CCC, nn. 1581-1584

# II

# Priests: Preachers of the Gospel

General Audience of Wednesday April 21, 1993

*Presbyters must not preach their own word, but the word of God that has been entrusted to the Church to be proclaimed in its integrity.*

1. In the Church we all are called to proclaim the Good News of Jesus Christ, to communicate it ever more fully to believers,[1] to make it known to non-believers.[2] No Christian can be excused from this task stemming from the very sacraments of Baptism and Confirmation and working under the impulse of the Holy Spirit. Thus it must be stated immediately that evangelization is not reserved to only one category of the Church's members.

Nevertheless, bishops are its principal agents and leaders for the entire Christian community, as we saw in discussing them. In this work they are assisted by presbyters, and to a certain degree by deacons, according to the Church's norms and practice, both in ancient times and in those of the "new evangelization."

2. For presbyters, it can be said that *proclaiming the word of God is the first task to be carried out,*[3] because the basis of personal and communal Christian life is faith, which results from the word of God and is nourished on this word.

The Second Vatican Council emphasizes this evangelizing mission and relates it to the formation of the People of God and to everyone's right to receive the Gospel message from priests.[4]

The need for this preaching is highlighted by St. Paul, who adds to Christ's command his own experience as an Apostle. In his work of evangelization, carried out in many regions and contexts, he noted that people did not believe because no one as yet had proclaimed the Good News to them. Although the way of salvation was now open to all, he observed that not everyone had yet been able to take advantage of it. Thus, he also explained the need for preaching because of Christ's command: "But how can they call on him in whom they have not believed? And how can they believe in him of whom they have not heard? And how can they hear without someone to preach? And how can people preach unless they are sent?"[5]

**Not Preachers of Their Own Experience**

The Apostle was concerned to communicate the word of God in abundance to those who had become believers. He himself said to the Thessalonians: "We treated each one of you as a father treats his children, exhorting and encouraging you and insisting that you conduct yourselves as worthy of the God who calls you. . . ."[6]

The Apostle urgently exhorts his disciple Timothy to carry out this ministry: "I charge you", he writes, "in the presence of God and of Christ . . . proclaim the word; be persistent whether it is convenient or inconvenient; convince, reprimand, encourage through all patience and teaching."[7] As for presbyters, he gives this rule: "Presbyters who preside well deserve double honor, *especially those who toil in preaching and teaching.*"[8]

3. The preaching of presbyters is not a mere exercise of the word that answers a personal need to express oneself and to communicate one's own thought, nor can it consist solely

in sharing one's personal experience. This psychological element, which can have a didactic-pastoral role, is neither the reason for nor the principal element in preaching. As the Fathers of the 1971 Synod of Bishops said: "The experiences of life, whether of men in general or of priests, which must be kept in mind and always interpreted in the light of the Gospel, cannot be either the sole or the principal norm of preaching."[9]

The mission of preaching is entrusted by the Church to presbyters as a sharing in Christ's mediation, to be exercised by virtue of and according to the demands of his mandate: priests, "in their degree of ministry, share in the office of the one Mediator, Christ,[10] and proclaim to all the divine word."[11] This expression cannot fail to make us reflect: it is a "divine word", which therefore is not "ours" and cannot be manipulated, changed or adapted at will, but must be proclaimed in its entirety.

Since the "divine word" has been entrusted to the Apostles and the Church, "Each priest shares in the special responsibility of preaching the whole of the word of God and of interpreting it according to the faith of the Church", as the Fathers also said at the 1971 Synod.[12]

4. The proclamation of the word takes place in close connection with the sacraments, through which Christ imparts and develops the life of grace.

In this regard it must also be noted that a good part of preaching, particularly today, takes place during the celebration of the sacraments and especially during holy Mass. It should also be observed that the proclamation already occurs through the administration of the sacraments, both because of the theological and catechetical richness of the liturgical texts and readings, given today in the vernacular and understandable by the people, and because of the ritual's pedagogical procedure.

### Preachers in Relation to the Sacraments

Doubtless, however, preaching must precede, accompany and crown the administration of the sacraments, in relation to the preparation necessary to receive them and to their fruitfulness in faith and life.

5. The Council recalled that proclaiming the divine word has the effect of producing and nourishing faith, and of contributing to the Church's development. It said: "For by the saving word of God faith is aroused in the heart of unbelievers and is nourished in the heart of believers. By this faith then the congregation of the faithful begins and grows."[13]

This principle must always be kept in mind: the goal of spreading, strengthening and increasing the faith must remain fundamental for everyone who preaches the Gospel, and thus for the priest who is particularly and so frequently called to exercise the "ministry of the word."

A preaching which would be a tissue of psychological themes related to the person, or taken up with raising problems without resolving them or causing doubts without indicating the source of Gospel light that can illumine the way for individuals and society, would not achieve the essential objective desired by the Savior. It would instead result in a source of disorientation for public opinion and of damage for believers themselves, whose right to know the true content of Revelation would thus be ignored.

### Preachers in Relation to the Gospel and the Church

6. Moreover, the Council has shown the breadth and variety of forms that the authentic proclamation of the Gospel can take, according to the Church's teaching and mandate to preachers: "Priests then owe it to everyone to share with them the truth of the Gospel in which they rejoice in the Lord. Therefore, whether by having their conversation heard among the gentiles they lead people to glorify God; or by openly preaching, proclaim the mystery of Christ to

unbelievers; or teach the Christian message or explain the Church's doctrine; or endeavor to treat of contemporary problems in the light of Christ's teaching—in every case their role is to teach not their own wisdom but the word of God and to issue an urgent invitation to all people to conversion and holiness."[14]

These then are the ways to teach the divine word according to the Church: the witness of one's life, which makes it possible to discover the power of God's love and gives persuasive force to the preacher's word; explicitly preaching the mystery of Christ to non-believers; catechesis and the ordered, organic exposition of the Church's doctrine; application of revealed truth to judging and solving practical cases.

7. This requirement of authentic and complete proclamation is not opposed to the principle of adapting preaching, which was particularly stressed by the Council.[15]

Clearly, the priest must above all ask himself, with a sense of responsibility and realistic evaluation, whether what he says in his preaching is understood by his listeners and whether it has an effect on the way they think and live. In addition, he should strive to take stock of his own preaching, the various needs of his listeners and the different reasons why they come together and seek his help.

Clearly he should know and recognize his talents and use them to good advantage, not to show off (which would simply destroy his credibility with his listeners), but the better to bring the divine word to human minds and hearts.

## Preachers Prompted by the Holy Spirit

More than to natural talents, however, the preacher must have recourse to those supernatural charisms that the history of the Church and sacred eloquence presents in so many holy preachers, and he will feel compelled to ask the Holy Spirit for the most appropriate, effective way to speak, act and dialogue with his audience.

All this is true as well for everyone who exercises the ministry of the word by writing, publishing, and by radio and television broadcasting. The use of these communications media too requires the preacher, lecturer, writer, religious entertainer and particularly the priest to call upon and have recourse to the Holy Spirit, the light who gives life to minds and hearts.

8. According to the Council's directives, the divine word should be proclaimed in all areas and at all levels of society, also taking non-believers into account: this means true atheists or, as is more often the case, agnostics, the indifferent or the heedless. In order to interest them it will be necessary to devise more appropriate measures. Here once again one need only point out the problem, which is serious and must be addressed with intelligent zeal and a calm attitude.

It can be useful for the priest to remember the wise consideration of the 1971 Synod of Bishops, which said: "By evangelization the minister of the word prepares the ways of the Lord with great patience and faith, conforming himself to the various conditions of individuals and peoples' lives."[16]

The ever necessary calling upon the Lord's grace and on the Holy Spirit, its divine steward, will be felt even more intensely in all those cases of (at least practical) atheism, agnosticism, ignorance and religious indifference, sometimes hostile prejudice and even animosity, which show the priest how inadequate are all human means for opening souls to God. Then, more than ever, he will experience the "mystery of empty hands", as it has been called; but for this very reason he will remember that St. Paul, almost crucified by similar experiences, always found new courage in the "power of God and the wisdom of God" present in Christ.[17]

St. Paul also reminded the Corinthians: "When I came among you it was in weakness and fear, and with much trepidation. My message and my preaching had none of the persuasive force of 'wise' argumentation, but the convincing power of the Spirit. As a consequence, your faith rests not on the wisdom of men but on the power of God."[18] Perhaps this is the important viaticum for today's preacher.

## NOTES

1. Cf. Col 3:16
2. Cf. 1 Pt 3:15
3. Cf. *Lumen gentium*, n. 28; *CCC*, n. 1564
4. Cf. *Presbyterorum Ordinis*, n. 4
5. Rom 10:14-15
6. 1 Thes 2:11-12
7. 2 Tm 4:1-2
8. 1 Tm 5:17
9. *Enchiridion Vaticanum*, IV, 1186
10. 1 Tim 2:5
11. *Ibid.*
12. *Enchiridion Vaticanum*, IV, 1183
13. *Presbyterorum ordinis* n. 4
14. *Ibid.*
15. *Ibid.*
16. *Enchiridion Vaticanum*, IV, 1184
17. Cf. 1 Cor 1:18-29
18. 1 Cor 2:3-5

# III

# Priests: Sanctifiers through the Sacraments

General Audience of Wednesday May 5, 1993

*Acting in the name of Christ, presbyters administer the sacraments which, by the power of the Holy Spirit, bestow the new life of grace.*

1. In speaking of the evangelizing mission of presbyters, we already saw that *in* the sacraments and *through* the sacraments a methodical and effective instruction on the word of God and the mystery of salvation can be imparted to the faithful. In fact, the priest's evangelizing mission is essentially related to the ministry of *sanctification through the sacraments.*[1]

The ministry of the word cannot be limited merely to the immediate, proper effect of the word. Evangelization is the first of those "apostolic endeavors" which, according to the Council, have as their goal "that all who are made children of God by faith and Baptism should come together to praise God in the midst of his Church, to take part in the Sacrifice and to eat the Lord's Supper."[2] And the 1971 Synod of Bishops stated: "The ministry of the word, if rightly understood, leads to the sacraments and to the Christian life, as it is practiced in the visible community of the Church and in the world."[3]

Any attempt to reduce the priestly ministry to preaching alone or to teaching would misunderstand an essential aspect of this ministry. The Council of Trent had already rejected the proposal to make the priesthood consist merely of the ministry of preaching the Gospel.[4] Since some, even recently, have too one-sidedly extolled the ministry of the word, the 1971 Synod of Bishops stressed the unbreakable covenant between word and sacrament. It said: "The sacraments are celebrated in conjunction with the proclamation of the word of God and thus develop faith by strengthening it with grace. They cannot be considered of slight importance, since through them the word is brought to fuller effect, namely communion in the mystery of Christ."[5]

### Preachers as Well as Ministers of the Sacraments

2. Regarding this unitary nature of the evangelizing mission and the sacramental ministry, the 1971 Synod did not hesitate to say that a division between evangelization and the celebration of the sacraments "would divide the heart of the Church to the point of imperiling the faith."[6]

The Synod, however, recognizes that for each priest there can be different ways of concretely applying this principle of unity, "for the exercise of the priestly ministry in practice needs to take different forms in order better to meet special or new situations in which the Gospel is to be proclaimed."[7]

A wise application of the principle of unity must also take into account the charisms each presbyter has received. If some have a particular talent for preaching or teaching they should use it for the good of the Church. It is helpful to recall here the case of St. Paul, who, although convinced of the need for Baptism and even having occasionally administered this sacrament, nevertheless thought of himself as having been sent to preach the Gospel and devoted his efforts primarily to this form of ministry.[8] In his preaching, however, he did not lose sight of the essential task of building up the community,[9] which this preaching must serve.

This means that today too, as throughout the history of the pastoral ministry, the division of labor can stress preaching or worship and the sacraments, according to the individual's abilities and the assessment of the situation. However, one can never doubt that for presbyters teaching and preaching, even at the highest academic and scholarly level, must always retain their purpose of serving the ministry of sanctification through the sacraments.

3. In any case, the important mission of sanctification entrusted to priests cannot be called into question. They can exercise this mission above all in the ministry of worship and the sacraments. Doubtless it is *a work carried out primarily by Christ,* as the 1971 Synod pointed out: "Salvation, which is effected through the sacraments, does not come from us but from God; this demonstrates the primacy of action of Christ, the one priest and mediator, in his body, which is the Church."[10]

In the present economy of salvation, however, Christ makes use of the presbyters' ministry to sanctify believers.[11] Acting in the name of Christ, the priest achieves effective sacramental action through the Holy Spirit, the Spirit of Christ, the principle and source of the holiness of the "new life."

The new life that the priest imparts, nurtures, restores and increases through the sacraments is a life of faith, hope and love. Faith is the basic divine gift: "This makes clear the great importance of preparation and of a disposition of faith on the part of the person who receives the sacraments; it also makes clear the necessity for a witness of faith on the part of the minister in his entire life and especially in the way he values and celebrates the sacraments themselves."[12]

### Exercising a Divinely Fruitful Ministry

The faith communicated by Christ through the sacraments is unfailingly accompanied by a "living hope,"[13] which instills in the hearts of the faithful a powerful dynamism of spiritual life, an impulse towards "what is above."[14] On the other hand, faith "works through love,"[15] the love of charity, which springs from the Savior's heart and flows into the sacraments to spread throughout Christian life.

4. The sacramental ministry of presbyters is thus endowed with a divine fruitfulness. The Council clearly recalled this.

Thus, by *Baptism* priests "introduce people into the People of God":[16] and, therefore they are responsible not only for worthily celebrating the rite, but also for providing a good preparation for it, by forming adults in the faith, and in regard to children, by educating the family to cooperate in the celebration.

Moreover, "in the spirit of Christ the Shepherd, they instruct them to submit their sins to the Church with a contrite heart in the sacrament of *Penance,* so that they may be daily more and more converted to the Lord, remembering his words, 'Repent, for the kingdom of heaven is at hand.'"[17] For this reason priests too must personally live with the attitude of men who acknowledge their own sins and their own need for forgiveness, in a communion of humility and repentance with the faithful. Thus they can more effectively show the greatness of the divine mercy and give heavenly comfort, as well as forgiveness, to those who feel oppressed by the weight of their guilt.

### Ministers to the Sick

In the sacrament of *Matrimony,* the presbyter is present as the one responsible for the celebration, testifying to the faith and receiving the consent on behalf of God, whom he represents as the Church's minister. In this way he participates deeply and vitally not only in the rite, but in the deepest dimension of the sacrament.

Finally, by the *Anointing of the Sick,* priests "relieve those who are ill."[18] It is a mission foreseen by St. James, who taught in his Letter: "Is anyone among you sick? He should summon the presbyters of the Church, and they should pray over him and anoint him with oil in the name of the Lord."[19] Knowing then that the sacrament of *Anointing* is meant to "relieve" and to bring purification and spiritual strength, the presbyter will feel the need to make sure that his presence brings the sick person the effective compassion of Christ and give witness to Jesus' kindness toward the sick, to whom he devoted such a large part of his evangelical mission.

5. This discussion of the dispositions which are necessary when one approaches the sacraments, celebrating them with awareness and a spirit of faith, will be completed in the catecheses that we shall devote to the sacraments. In the next catecheses we will discuss another aspect of the priest's mission in the sacramental ministry: the worship of God, which is carried out especially in the Eucharist. For now let us say that this is the most important element of his role in the Church, the principal reason for his ordination, the purpose that gives meaning and joy to his life.

## NOTES

1. Cf. CCC, n. 893
2. *Sacrosanctum Concilium,* n. 10
3. *Enchiridion Vaticanum,* IV, 1179
4. Cf. DS 1771
5. *Enchiridion Vaticanum,* IV, 1180
6. Cf. *Enchiridion Vaticanum,* IV, 1181
7. *Enchiridion Vaticanum,* IV, 1182
8. Cf. 1 Cor 1:14-17
9. Cf. 1 Cor 3:10
10. Cf. *Enchiridion Vaticanum,* IV, 1187 and cf. also the Post-Synodal Apostolic Exhortation *Pastores dabo vobis,* n. 12
11. Cf. *Presbyterorum ordinis,* n. 5
12. Cf. *Enchiridion Vaticanum,* IV, 1188
13. 1 Pt. 1:3
14. Col 3:1-2
15. Gal 5:6

16. *Presbyterorum ordinis,* n. 5
17. Mt 4:17 and *Presbyterorum ordinis,* n. 5
18. *Presbyterorum ordinis,* n. 5
19. Jas 5:14

# IV

# Priests: Ordained to Celebrate Mass

General Audience of Wednesday May 12, 1993

*Presbyters carry out their sacred ministry above all in the Eucharist: acting in the person of Christ, they re-present his eternal sacrifice.*

1. The complete dimension of the presbyter's mission in relation to the Eucharist is understood if one considers that this sacrament is primarily the renewal, at the altar, of the sacrifice of the cross, the central moment in the work of redemption. Christ, the Priest and Victim, is as such the artisan of universal salvation, in obedience to the Father. He is the one High Priest of the new and eternal covenant, who by accomplishing our salvation offers perfect worship to the Father, a worship which ancient celebrations of the Old Testament merely prefigured.

By the sacrifice of his own blood on the cross, Christ "entered once for all into the sanctuary, thus obtaining eternal redemption."[1] Thus he abolished every ancient sacrifice in order to establish a new one by offering himself to the Father's will.[2] "By this 'will', we have been consecrated through the offering of the body of Jesus Christ once for all. . . . For by one offering he has made perfect forever those who are being consecrated."[3]

In sacramentally renewing the sacrifice of the cross, the presbyter reopens that source of salvation in the Church and the entire world.[4]

2. For this reason the 1971 Synod of Bishops, in accord with the documents of Vatican II, pointed out: "The priestly ministry reaches its summit in the celebration of the Eucharist, which is the source and center of the Church's unity."[5]

The Dogmatic Constitution on the Church asserts: "It is in Eucharistic cult or in the *Eucharistic assembly* of the faithful that they exercise in a supreme degree their sacred functions; there, acting in the person of Christ and proclaiming his mystery they unite the votive offerings of the faithful to the sacrifice of Christ their head, and in the sacrifice of the Mass they make present again and apply, until the coming of the Lord, the unique sacrifice of the New Testament, that namely of Christ offering himself once for all a spotless victim to the Father."[6]

In this regard, the Decree *Presbyterorum ordinis* makes two fundamental assertions:

- The community is gathered by the proclamation of the Gospel so that all can make a spiritual offering of themselves;
- The spiritual sacrifice of the faithful is made perfect through union with Christ's sacrifice, offered in an unbloody, sacramental manner by the hands of the priests. Their whole priestly ministry draws its force from this one sacrifice.[7]

### Called to Mystical Identification with Christ

This shows the connection between the ministerial priesthood and the common priesthood of the faithful. It also shows how the priest, among all the faithful, is especially called to identify himself mystically—as well as sacramentally—with Christ, in order to be himself in some way *Sacerdos et Hostia*, according to the beautiful expression of St. Thomas Aquinas.[8]

3. In the Eucharist the presbyter reaches the high point of his ministry when he pronounces Jesus' words: "This is my body. . . . This is the cup of my blood. . . ." These words concretize the greatest exercise of that power which enables the priest to make present the sacrifice of Christ. Then the community is truly built up and developed—in a sacramental way and, thus, with divine efficacy.

The Eucharist is indeed the sacrament of communion and unity, as was asserted by the 1971 Synod of Bishops and more recently by the Letter of the Congregation for the Doctrine of the Faith on some aspects of the Church understood as communion.[9]

This is how one explains the piety and fervor with which saintly priests—about whom hagiography tells us abundantly—always celebrated Mass, not hesitating to make adequate preparation beforehand and afterwards to make suitable acts of thanksgiving. In order to help with making these acts the Missal offers appropriate prayers, often laudably printed on special cards in sacristies. We also know that on the theme of *Sacerdos et Hostia* various works of priestly spirituality have been written and can always be recommended to priests.

4. Here is another essential point of Eucharistic-priestly theology, the subject of our catechesis: the whole ministry and all the sacraments are directed towards the Eucharist, in which "the whole spiritual good of the Church is contained,[10] namely Christ himself our Pasch and the living Bread which gives life to men through his flesh—that flesh which is given life and gives life through the Holy Spirit. Thus men are invited and led to offer themselves, their works and all creation with Christ."[11]

## Deeply Linked to the Eucharist

In the celebration of the Eucharist, therefore, the greatest participation takes place in the perfect worship which Christ the High Priest gives to the Father by representing and expressing the whole created order. The presbyter, who sees and recognizes that his life is thus deeply linked to the Eucharist, feels the horizons of his spirit broadened on a global scale, embracing even heaven and earth, and is also aware of the increased need and responsibility to impart this treasure—"the whole spiritual good of the Church"— to the community.

5. Therefore, in the projects and programmes of his pastoral ministry, he keeps in mind that the sacramental life of the faithful is directed towards the Eucharist[12] and he will see to it that Christian formation aims at the active, conscious participation of the faithful in the Eucharistic celebration.

Today it is necessary to rediscover the central importance of this celebration in Christian life and, thus, in the apostolate. The data on the Mass attendance of the faithful is not encouraging: although the zeal of many priests has led to a generally fervent and active participation, the attendance percentages remain low. It is true that in this area, more than in any other regarding the interior life, the value of statistics is quite relative; furthermore, it is not the structured, outward expression of worship that proves its real worth.

Nevertheless, one cannot ignore the fact that outward worship is normally a logical consequence of what is inside,[13] and, in the case of Eucharistic worship, it is a consequence of faith itself in Christ the Priest and his redeeming sacrifice. Nor would it be wise to minimize the importance of the celebration of worship by citing the fact that the vitality of the Christian faith is shown by conduct in complete conformity with the Gospel, rather than by ritual gestures.

In fact, the Eucharistic celebration is not a mere ritual gesture: it is a sacrament, i.e., an intervention of Christ himself who communicates to us the dynamism of his love. It would be a pernicious illusion to claim that one is acting in accordance with the Gospel without receiving its strength from Christ himself in the Eucharist, the sacrament he instituted for this purpose. Such a claim would be a radically anti-Gospel attitude of self-sufficiency.

The Eucharist gives Christians greater strength to live according to the demands of the Gospel; it makes them more fully members of the ecclesial community to which they belong; it renews and enriches in them the joy of communion in the Church.

### Teachers of the Eucharist

Therefore, the priest will make every effort to encourage participation in the Eucharist by catechesis, pastoral exhortation and the excellent quality of the celebration in its liturgical and ceremonial aspect. He will thus succeed, as the Council stresses,[14] in teaching the faithful to offer the divine victim to God the Father in the sacrifice of the Mass and, in union with this victim, to make an offering of their own life in service to their brothers and sisters.

The faithful will also learn to seek pardon for their sins, to meditate on the word of God, to pray with sincere hearts for all the needs of the Church and the world and to put all their trust in Christ the Savior.

6. Finally, I want to mention that the priest has the mission to promote the worship of the Eucharistic presence outside of the celebration of Mass too, by striving to make his own church a Christian "house of prayer": i.e., one in which, according to the Council, "the presence of the Son of God, our Savior, offered for us on the sacrificial altar for the help and consolation of the faithful is worshiped."[15]

This house must be a worthy place for prayer and sacred functions both for its good order, cleanliness, the neatness with which it is maintained, and for the artistic beauty of its environment, which has a great importance for the way it forms and inspires prayer. For this reason the Council recommends that the priest "properly cultivate liturgical knowledge and art."[16]

I have called attention to these aspects because they too belong to the complex picture of a good "care of souls" on the part of priests, particularly parish priests and all those responsible for churches and other places of worship.

In any case, I stress the close connection between the priesthood and the Eucharist, as the Church teaches us, and I reaffirm with conviction and deep spiritual joy that the presbyter is above all *the man of the Eucharist:* Christ's servant and minister in this sacrament, in which—according to the Council, summarizing the teaching of the ancient Fathers and doctors—"the whole spiritual good of the Church is contained."[17]

Every priest, at any level, in any area of work, is the servant and minister of the paschal mystery accomplished on the cross and lived anew on the altar for the redemption of the world.

## NOTES

1. Heb 9:12
2. Cf. Ps 40 [39]:9
3. Heb 10:10,14
4. Cf. CCC, nn. 1362-1372
5. *Enchiridion Vaticanum,* IV, 1166; cf. *Ad Gentes,* n. 39
6. *Lumen gentium,* n. 28, cf. CCC n. 1566
7. Cf. *Presbyterorum ordinis,* n. 2; cf. CCC, n. 1566
8. Cf. *Summa Theol.,* III, q. 83, a. 1, *ad* 3
9. Cf. *Communionis notio,* n. 11
10. Cf. St. Thomas Aquinas, *Summa Theol.,* III, q. 65, a. 3, *ad 1;* q. 79, a. 1
11. *Presbyterorum ordinis,* n. 5
12. Cf. *Presbyterorum ordinis,* n. 5
13. Cf. St. Thomas Aquinas, *Summa Theol.,* III, q. 81, a. 7
14. *Presbyterorum ordinis,* n. 5
15. *Ibid.*
16. *Ibid.*
17. *Ibid.*

# V

# Priests: Shepherds to the Community

General Audience of Wednesday May 19, 1993

*In carrying out his pastoral ministry, the priest must strive to promote the spiritual and ecclesial maturity of the community entrusted to him.*

1. In the previous catecheses we explained the presbyters' task as coworkers of the bishops in the area of teaching authority (instructing) and sacramental ministry (sanctifying). Today we will speak of their cooperation *in the pastoral governance of the community.* For priests as well as for bishops it is a sharing in the third aspect of Christ's threefold *munus* (prophetic, priestly, royal): a reflection of the high priesthood of Christ, the one Mediator between God and men, the one Teacher, the one Shepherd. In an ecclesial perspective pastoral work consists principally in the *service of unity,* that is, in ensuring the union of all in the Body of Christ which is the Church.[1]

2. In this perspective the Council says: "Priests exercise the function of Christ as Pastor and Head in proportion to their share of authority. In the name of the bishop they gather the family of God as a brotherhood endowed with the spirit of unity and lead it in Christ through the Spirit to God the Father."[2] This is the essential purpose of their activity as

pastors and of the authority conferred on them so that they may exercise it at their level of responsibility: leading the community entrusted to them to the full development of its spiritual and ecclesial life. The *presbyter-pastor* [i.e., shepherd] must exercise this authority by modeling himself on Christ the *Good Shepherd,* who did not impose it with external coercion but by forming the community through the interior action of his Spirit.

He wanted to share his burning love with the group of disciples and with all those who accepted his message, in order to give life to a "community of love", which at the right moment he also established visibly as the Church. As coworkers of the bishops, the successors of the Apostles, presbyters too fulfill their mission in the visible community by enlivening it with charity so that it may live in the Spirit of Christ.

### Responsible for the Organic Functioning of the Community

3. It is a demand intrinsic to the pastoral mission, whose inspiration is not governed by the priest's desires and personal opinions, but by the teaching of the Gospel, as the Council says: "They should act towards people not according to what may please men, but according to the demands of Christian doctrine and life."[3]

The presbyter is responsible for the organic functioning of the community. To fulfill this task the bishop gives him a necessary share in his authority. It is his responsibility to ensure that the various services, indispensable for the good of all, are carried out harmoniously; to find appropriate assistance for the liturgy, catechesis and the spiritual support of married couples; to foster the development of various spiritual and apostolic associations or "movements" in harmony and cooperation; to organize charitable aid for the needy, the sick and immigrants.

At the same time he must ensure and promote the community's union with the Bishop and the Pope.

4. The community dimension of pastoral care, however, cannot overlook *the needs of the individual faithful.* As we read in the Council: "It is the priests' part as instructors in the faith to see to it either personally or through others that each member of the faithful shall be led in the Holy Spirit to the full development of his own vocation in accordance with the Gospel teaching, to sincere and active charity and to the liberty with which Christ has set us free."[4]

The Council stresses the need to help each member of the faithful to discover his specific vocation as a proper, characteristic task of the pastor who wants to respect and promote each one's personality. One could say that by his own example Jesus himself, the Good Shepherd who "calls his own sheep by name,"[5] has set the standard of individual pastoral care: knowledge and a relationship of friendship with individual persons.

It is the presbyter's task to help each one to utilize well his own gift and rightly to exercise the freedom that comes from Christ's salvation as St. Paul urges.[6]

Everything must be directed towards practicing "a sincere and active charity." This means that "Christians must also be trained so as not to live only for themselves. Rather, according to the demands of the new law of charity, everyone as he has received grace ought to minister it one to another, and in this way all should carry out their duties in a Christian way in the human community."[7]

Therefore, the priest's mission includes calling to mind the obligations of charity; showing the applications of charity in social life; fostering an atmosphere of unity with respect for differences; encouraging programmes and works of charity, by which great opportunities become available to the faithful, especially through the new emphasis on volunteer work, consciously provided as a good use of free time, and in many cases, as a choice of life.

## Champions of the Poor, the Sick, and the Young

5. The presbyter is also called to be involved personally in works of charity, sometimes even in extraordinary forms, as has happened in the past and does so today as well. Here I especially want to underscore that simple, habitual, almost unassuming but constant and generous charity which is manifested not so much in huge projects—for which many do not have the talent and vocation—but in the daily practice of goodness, which helps, supports and comforts according to each one's capacity.

Clearly the principal concern, and one could say the preference, must be for "the poor and weaker ones, to whom the preaching of the Gospel is given as a sign of messianic mission"[8] for "the sick and dying", to whom the priest should be especially devoted, "visiting them and comforting them in the Lord";[9] for "young people, who must be looked after with special diligence"; as well as for "married couples and parents."[10]

In particular, the priest must devote his time, energy and talents to young people, who are the hope of the community, in order to foster their Christian education and their growth in living according to the Gospel.

The Council also commends to the presbyter's care "catechumens and neophytes, who must be gradually educated in knowing and living the Christian life."[11]

6. Lastly, attention must be paid to the need to overcome a too limited vision of the local community and every particularist and, as is usually said, "parochial" attitude to foster instead the community spirit that is open to the horizons of the universal Church. Even when the presbyter must devote his time and concern to the local community entrusted to him, as is the case especially for parish priests and their closest coworkers, his heart must remain open to the "fields ripe for the harvest" beyond all borders, as the universal dimension of the spirit and as the personal participation in the Church's missionary tasks, and as zeal in promoting

the cooperation of his community with the necessary spiritual and material aid.[12]

"In virtue of the sacrament of Orders", the *Catechism of the Catholic Church* states, "priests share in the universal dimension of the mission entrusted by Christ to the Apostles. 'The spiritual gift which priests have received in ordination does not prepare them merely for a limited and circumscribed mission but for the fullest, in fact, the universal mission of salvation to the end of the earth,'[13] 'being prepared in spirit to preach the Gospel everywhere'."[14]

### Dependent on the Eucharist for Inspiration and Strength

7. In any case, everything depends on the Eucharist, which contains the vital principle of pastoral leadership. As the Council says: "No Christian community is built up which does not grow from and hinge on the celebration of the Holy Eucharist. From this all education for community spirit must begin."[15] The Eucharist is the source of unity and the most perfect expression of the union of all the Christian community's members. It is the presbyters' task to ensure that this is really so.

Unfortunately, it sometimes happens that Eucharistic celebrations are not expressions of unity. Each person attends individually, ignoring the others. With great pastoral charity, priests will remind everyone of St. Paul's teaching: "Because the loaf of bread is one, we, though many, *are one body*, for we all partake of the one loaf", which is "a participation in the body of Christ."[16] Awareness of this union in the body of Christ will encourage a life of charity and effective solidarity.

The Eucharist, therefore, is the vital principle of the Church as the community of Christ's members: here pastoral leadership finds its inspiration, strength and extent.

# NOTES

1. *Pastores dabo vobis*, n. 16
2. *Presbyterorum ordinis*, n. 6
3. *Ibid.*
4. *Ibid.*
5. Cf. Jn 10:3-4
6. Cf. Gal 4:3; 5:1,13; cf. also Jn 8:36
7. *Presbyterorum ordinis* n. 6
8. *Ibid.*
9. *Ibid.*
10. *Ibid.*
11. *Ibid.*
12. Cf. *Redemptoris missio* n. 67, *Pastores dabo vobis* n. 32
13. *Presbyterorum ordinis*, n. 10
14. *Optatum totius*, n. 20 and CCC, n. 1565
15. *Presbyterorum ordinis*, n. 6
16. 1 Cor 10:16-17

# VI

# Priests: Consecrated to God

General Audience of Wednesday May 26, 1993

*The Second Vatican Council clearly recognized the importance of priestly holiness for renewing the Church and spreading the Gospel.*

1. All of Christian tradition, based on Sacred Scripture, speaks of the priest as a "man of God", a man consecrated to God. *Homo Dei:* this definition is valid for every Christian, but St. Paul refers it particularly to Bishop Timothy, his disciple, when he recommends the use of Sacred Scripture to him.[1] It is appropriate to the presbyter as well as to the bishop, by reason of his special consecration to God. In truth, a person already receives a first, basic consecration in Baptism, with deliverance from evil and entry into a special state of belonging ontologically and psychologically to God.[2] Priestly ordination confirms and deepens this state of consecration, as the 1971 Synod of Bishops recalled when it referred to the priesthood of Christ shared by the presbyter through the anointing of the Holy Spirit.[3]

Here the Synod took up again the teaching of Vatican II which, after reminding presbyters of their duty to strive for perfection by virtue of their baptismal "consecration", added: "Priests are bound by a special reason to acquire this perfection. They are consecrated to God in a new way in their ordination and are made the living instruments of Christ the Eternal Priest, and so are enabled to accomplish throughout all time that wonderful work of his which with supernatural efficacy restored the whole human race."[4] Pius XI recommended the same in his Encyclical *Ad catholici sacerdotii* of December 20, 1935.[5]

### Imitators of Christ

According to the faith of the Church, priestly ordination not only confers a new mission in the Church, a ministry, but a new "consecration" of the person, one linked to the character imprinted by the sacrament of Orders as a spiritual, indelible sign of a special belonging to Christ in being and, consequently, in acting. The perfection required of the presbyter is thus commensurate with his sharing in the priesthood of Christ as the author of redemption: the minister cannot be exempted from reproducing in himself the sentiments, inner tendencies and intentions, the spirit of sacrifice to the Father and of service to the brethren that is proper to the "principal Agent."

2. As a result the priest has a sort of mastery of grace, which allows him to enjoy union with Christ and at the same time to be devoted to the pastoral service of his brothers and sisters. As the Council says, since the priest "in his own way assumes the person of Christ he is endowed with a special grace. By this grace he, through his service of the people committed to his care and all the People of God, is able the better to pursue the perfection of Christ, whose place he takes. The human weakness of his flesh is remedied by the holiness of him who became for us a high priest 'holy, innocent undefiled, separated from sinners'."[6] In this condition the priest is bound to a special *imitation of Christ the Priest*, which is the result of the special grace of Orders: the grace of *union with Christ the Priest and Victim* and, by virtue of this same union, the grace of *good pastoral service to his brothers and sisters.*

In this regard it is helpful to recall the example of St. Paul. He lived as an entirely consecrated apostle, he who was "taken possession of by Christ Jesus", and left everything to live in union with him.[7] He felt so filled with Christ's life that he could say in complete sincerity: "Yet I live, no longer I but Christ lives in me."[8] Nevertheless after alluding to the extraordinary favors he had received as a "man in Christ,"[9] he also suffered a thorn in the flesh, a trial from which he was never freed. Despite a triple request made to the Lord, he heard him respond: "My grace is sufficient for you, for power is made perfect in weakness."[10]

In the light of this example, the presbyter can better understand that he must strive to live fully his own consecration by remaining united to Christ and allowing himself to be imbued with his Spirit, despite the experience of his own human limitations. These will not prevent him from carrying out his ministry, because he is favored with a "grace that is sufficient for him." It is in this grace, then, that the priest must put his trust; it is to this grace that he must have recourse, knowing that he can thus strive for perfection in the hope of continually increasing in holiness.

### Men of Penitential Spirit

3. His sharing in Christ's priesthood cannot fail to arouse in the presbyter a sacrificial spirit too, a type of *pondus crucis*, the burden of the cross, which is expressed especially in mortification. As the Council says: "Christ, whom the Father sanctified or consecrated and sent into the world, 'gave himself for us to redeem us from all iniquity and to purify for himself a people of his own who are zealous for good deeds'[11]. . . . In a similar way, priests, who are consecrated by the anointing of the Holy Spirit and sent by Christ, mortify the works of the flesh in themselves and dedicate themselves completely to the service of the people, and so are able, in the holiness with which they have been enriched in Christ, to make progress towards the perfect man."[12]

This is the *ascetical* aspect of the way of perfection, which for the priest cannot be lacking in renunciation and struggle against every sort of desire and yearning that would induce him to seek the good things of this world, thus compromising his interior progress. This is the "spiritual combat" of which the ascetical masters speak and which is required of every follower of Christ, but especially of every minister in the work of the cross, called to reproduce in himself the image of him who is *Sacerdos et Hostia*.

4. Obviously, one always needs to be open and responsive to the grace which itself comes from him who begets "any measure of desire or achievement"[13], but who also demands that one use the means of mortification and self-discipline without which one remains impervious soil. The ascetical tradition has always pointed out—and in a certain sense prescribed— to priests certain means of sanctification, particularly the appropriate celebration of Mass, the punctual recitation of the Divine Office ("not to be mishandled", as St. Alphonsus M. de' Liguori recommended), visits to the Blessed Sacrament, daily recitation of the Rosary, daily meditation and periodic reception of sacramental Penance. These practices are still valid and indispensable.

Particular importance must be given to the sacrament of Penance, the careful reception of which helps the presbyter to have a realistic image of himself, with the resulting awareness that he too is a poor, weak man, a sinner among sinners, one in need of forgiveness. He thus acquires "truth about himself" and is led to have confident recourse to the divine mercy.[14]

### Men of Personal Holiness

In addition, it must always be remembered that as the Council says: "Priests will acquire holiness in their own distinctive way by exercising their functions sincerely and tirelessly in the Spirit of Christ."[15] Thus, the proclamation of the word encourages them to achieve in themselves what they teach to others. The celebration of the sacraments strengthens them in faith and in union with Christ. The whole pastoral ministry develops their charity: "While they govern and shepherd the People of God they are encouraged by the love of the Good Shepherd to give their lives for their sheep. They, too, are prepared for the supreme sacrifice." Their ideal will be to achieve unity of life in Christ, integrating prayer and ministry, contemplation and action, because they continually seek the Father's will and the gift of themselves for the flock.[17]

5. Moreover, it is a source of courage and joy for the presbyter to know that his personal commitment to sanctification helps make his ministry effective. In fact, as the Council recalls: "While it is possible for God's grace to carry out the work of salvation through unworthy ministers, yet God ordinarily prefers to show his wonders through those men who are more submissive to the impulse and guidance of the Holy Spirit and who, because of their intimate union with Christ and their holiness of life, are able to say with St. Paul: 'It is no longer I who live, but Christ who lives in me'."[18]

When the priest recognizes that he is called to serve as the *instrument of Christ,* he feels the need to live in intimate *union with Christ* in order to be a *valid instrument* of the "principal Agent." Therefore, he seeks to reproduce in himself the "consecrated life" (the sentiments and virtues) of the one, eternal Priest who shares with him not only his power, but also his state of sacrifice for accomplishing the divine plan. *Sacerdos et Hostia.*

6. I will finish with a recommendation of the Council: "This sacred Council, in the hope of attaining its pastoral objectives of interior renewal, of worldwide diffusion of the Gospel, and of dialogue with the modern world, issues the strongest exhortation to all priests to strive always by the use of all suitable means commended by the Church towards that greater holiness that will make them daily more

effective instruments for the service of all God's People."[19] This is the greatest contribution we can make to building up the Church as the beginning of God's kingdom in the world.

## NOTES

1. Cf. 2 Tm 3:16
2. Cf. St. Thomas Aquinas, *Summa Theol.*, II-II, q. 81, a. 8
3. Cf. *Enchiridion Vaticanum*, IV, 1200-1201
4. *Presbyterorum ordinis*, n. 12
5. Cf. *MS* 28 [1936]:10
6. Heb 7:26, *Presbyterorum ordinis*, n. 12 cf. *Pastores dabo vobis* n. 20
7. Cf. Phil 3:7-12
8. Gal 2:20
9. 2 Cor 12:2
10. 2 Cor 12:9
11. Ti 2:14
12. *Presbyterorum ordinis*, n. 12
13. Phil 2:1 3
14. Cf. *Reconciliatio et Paenitentia*, n. 31; *Pastores dabo vobis*, n. 26
15. *Presbyterorum ordinis*, n. 13
16. *Ibid.*
17. *Ibid.* n. 14
18. Gal 2:20, *Presbyterorum ordinis*, n. 12
19. *Presbyterorum ordinis*, n. 12

# VII

# Priests:
# Devoted to Prayer

General Audience of Wednesday June 2, 1993

*Because the priest is sacramentally configured to Christ, he must be a man of prayer, as one ordained to continue the High Priest's mission.*

1. Today we return to some ideas already mentioned in the preceding catechesis in order to underscore further the demands and repercussions stemming from the reality of being a *man consecrated to God,* as we have described them. In a word we can say that, consecrated in the image of Christ, the priest must be a *man of prayer* like Christ himself. This concise definition embraces the whole spiritual life that gives the presbyter a true Christian identity, defines him as a priest and is the motivating principle of his apostolate.

The Gospel shows Jesus in prayer at every important moment of his mission. His public life, inaugurated at his Baptism, began with prayer.[1] Even in the more intense periods of teaching the crowds, he reserved long intervals for prayer.[2] Before choosing the Twelve he spent a night in prayer.[3] He prayed before asking his Apostles for a profession of faith;[4] he prayed alone on the mountain after the miracle of the loaves;[5] he prayed before teaching his disciples to pray;[6] he prayed before the extraordinary revelation of the Transfiguration, having ascended the mountain precisely to pray;[7] he prayed before performing some miracles;[8] he prayed at the Last Supper to entrust his future and that of his Church to the Father.[9]

In Gethsemane he offered the Father the sorrowful prayer of his afflicted and almost horrified soul,[10] and on the cross he made his last invocations, full of anguish,[11] but also of trustful abandon.[12] It could be said that Christ's whole mission was animated with prayer, from the beginning of his messianic ministry to the supreme priestly act: the sacrifice of the cross, which was made in prayer.

**Diligent in Personal Prayer**

2. Those called to share Christ's mission and sacrifice find in his example the incentive to give prayer its rightful place in their lives, as the foundation, root and guarantee of holiness in action. Indeed, we learn from Jesus that a fruitful exercise of the priesthood is impossible without prayer, which protects the presbyter from the danger of neglecting the interior life for the sake of action and from the temptation of so throwing himself into work as to be lost in it.

After stating that "the norm of priestly life" is found in Christ's consecration, the source of his Apostles' consecration, the 1971 Synod of Bishops also applied the norm to prayer in these words: "Following the example of Christ who was continually in prayer, and led by the Holy Spirit in whom we cry, 'Abba, Father', priests should give themselves to the contemplation of the word of God and daily take the opportunity to examine the events of life in the light of the Gospel, so that having become faithful and attentive hearers of the *Word* they may become true ministers of the *word*. Let them be assiduous in personal prayer, in the Liturgy of the Hours, in frequent reception of the sacrament of Penance and especially in devotion to the mystery of the Eucharist."[13]

3. For its part, the Second Vatican Council did not fail to remind priests of the need to be habitually united to Christ, and to this end it recommended diligence in prayer: "In various ways, in particular through the approved practice of mental prayer and the different forms of vocal prayer which they freely choose to practice, priests are to seek and perseveringly ask of God the true spirit of adoration which unites them with Christ, the Mediator of the covenant."[14] As we see among the possible forms of prayer the Council calls attention to *mental prayer,* which is a way to pray that is free from rigid formulas, does not require the recitation of words and responds to the Holy Spirit's lead in contemplating the divine mystery.

## Devoted to Contemplation

4. The 1971 Synod of Bishops insisted particularly on "contemplation of the word of God."[15] One should not be frightened by the word "contemplation" and the spiritual commitment it entails. It could be said that, independently of forms and life-styles, among which the "contemplative life" remains the most splendid jewel of Christ's Bride, the Church, the call to hear and meditate on the word of God in a contemplative spirit is valid for everyone, so that hearts and minds may be nourished on it. This helps the priest to develop a way of thinking and of looking at the world with wisdom, in the perspective of its supreme purpose: God and his plan of salvation. The Synod says: "To examine the events of life in the light of the Gospel."[16]

Herein lies supernatural wisdom, above all as a gift of the Holy Spirit, who makes it possible to exercise good judgement in the light of the "ultimate reasons", the "eternal things." Wisdom thus becomes the principal factor in identifying with Christ in thought, judgement, the evaluation of any matter however large or small, so that the priest (like every Christian only more so) reflects the light, obedience to the Father, practical zeal, rhythm of prayer and action and, one could almost say, the spiritual breath of Christ.

This goal can be reached by allowing oneself to be guided by the Holy Spirit in meditating on the Gospel, which fosters a deeper union with Christ, helps one to enter ever further into the Master's thought and strengthens the *personal* attachment to him. If the priest is diligent in this he remains more easily in a state of conscious joy arising from his perception of the intimate, personal fulfilment of the word of God, which he must teach others. In fact, as the Council says of presbyters, "by seeking more effective ways of conveying to others what they have meditated on they will savor more profoundly the 'unsearchable riches of Christ' and 'the manifold wisdom of God'."[17]

Let us pray the Lord to grant us a great number of priests who in their prayer life discover, assimilate and taste the wisdom of God,[18] and like the Apostle Paul, sense the supernatural inclination to proclaim and bestow it as the true reason for their apostolate.[19]

5. In speaking of the priests' prayer, the Council also mentions and recommends the Liturgy of the Hours, which joins the priest's personal prayer to that of the Church. "In reciting the Divine Office", it says, "they lend their voice to the Church which perseveres in prayer in the name of the whole human race, in union with Christ who 'always lives to make intercession for them'."[20]

By virtue of the mission of representation and intercession entrusted to him, the presbyter is formally obliged to this form of "official" prayer, delegated by the Church and made in the name not only of believers but of all mankind and, one could say, of the whole universe.[21] Sharing in Christ's priesthood, he makes intercession for the needs of the Church, the world and every human being, knowing that he represents and expresses the universal voice that sings the glory of God and seeks the salvation of mankind.

## In Need of Frequent Reception of the Sacrament of Penance

6. It is good to recall that, in order to give greater assurance to their prayer life and to strengthen and renew it by drawing on its sources, priests are asked by the Council to devote (in addition to time for the daily practice of prayer) longer periods to intimacy with Christ: "They should be glad to take time for spiritual retreat and should have a high regard for spiritual direction."[22] This will serve as a friendly and fatherly hand to help them on their way. As they experience the benefits of this guidance, they will be all the more ready to offer this help, in turn, to those who are entrusted to their pastoral ministry. This will be a great resource for many people today, especially young people, and will play a decisive role in solving the problem of vocations, as the experience of so many generations of priests and religious show.

In the preceding catechesis we already mentioned the importance of the sacrament of Penance. The Council urges the presbyter to make "frequent use" of it. Obviously whoever exercises the ministry of reconciling Christians with the Lord through the sacrament of forgiveness must himself have recourse to this sacrament. He will be the first to acknowledge that he is a sinner and to believe in the divine pardon expressed by sacramental absolution. In administering the sacrament of forgiveness, this awareness of being a sinner will help him better to understand sinners.

Does not the Letter to the Hebrews say of the priest, taken from among men: "He is able to deal patiently with the ignorant and erring, for he himself is beset by weakness?"[24] In addition, the personal use of the sacrament of Penance motivates the priest to make himself more available to administering this sacrament to the faithful who request it. This too is an urgent pastoral need in our day.

7. The presbyters' prayer, however reaches its apex in the Eucharistic celebration, "their principal function."[23] This is

such an important point for the priest's prayer life that I want to devote the next catechesis to it.

## NOTES

1. Lk 3:21
2. Mk 1:35; Lk 5:16
3. Lk 6:12
4. Lk 9:18
5. Mt 14:23 Mk 6:46
6. Lk 11:1
7. Lk 9:28
8. Jn 11:41-42
9. Jn 17
10. Mk 15:35-39 and par.
11. Mt 27:46
12. Lk 23:46
13. Cf. *Enchiridion Vaticanum*, IV, 1201
14. *Presbyterorum ordinis*, n. 18
15. Cf. *Enchiridion Vaticanum*, IV, 1201
16. Cf. *Enchiridion Vaticanum*, IV, 1201
17. Eph. 3:8, 10 and *Presbyterorum ordinis*, n. 13
18. Cf. *ibid.*
19. Cf. *Pastores dabo vobis*, n. 47
20. Heb 7:25, *Presbyterorum ordinis* n. 13
21. Cf. *CIC*, can. 1174, 1
22. *Presbyterorum ordinis*, n. 18
23. *Ibid.* n. 13
24. Heb 5:2

# VIII

# Priests: Spiritually Rooted in the Eucharist

General Audience of Wednesday June 9, 1993

*In the Eucharist priests are united with the Lord in his thanksgiving to the Father, grow in pastoral charity, and learn to praise God.*

The eyes of believers all over the world are turned these days to Seville where, as you know, the International Eucharistic Congress is being celebrated, and where I shall have the joy of going next Saturday and Sunday.

At the beginning of today's meeting, in which we shall reflect on the value of the Eucharist in the spiritual life of the presbyter, I paternally invite you to join in spirit in that great, important celebration, which calls everyone to a genuine renewal of faith and devotion towards the true presence of Christ in the Eucharist.

1. The catecheses which we are developing on the spiritual life of the priest especially concern presbyters, but they are addressed to all the faithful. It is indeed good that everyone should know the Church's doctrine on the priesthood and what she desires of those who, having received it, are conformed to the sublime image of Christ, the eternal Priest and most pure Victim of the salvific sacrifice.

That image is developed in the *Letters to the Hebrews* and in other texts of the Apostles and Evangelists, and it has been handed on faithfully in the Church's tradition of thought and life. Today too it is necessary for the clergy to be faithful to that image, which mirrors the living truth of Christ the Priest and Victim.

### Privileged to Celebrate the Mass Daily

2. The reproduction of that image in priests is attained primarily through their life-giving participation in the Eucharistic mystery, to which the Christian priesthood is essentially ordered and linked. The Council of Trent emphasized that the bond between the priesthood and sacrifice comes from the will of Christ, who conferred upon his ministers "the power to consecrate, to offer and to distribute his Body and his Blood."[1] In this there is a mystery of communion with Christ in *being* and *doing,* which must be translated into a spiritual life imbued with faith in and love for the Eucharist.

The priest is quite aware that he cannot count on his own efforts to achieve the purposes of his ministry, but rather that he is called to serve as an instrument of the victorious action of Christ whose sacrifice, made present on the altars, obtains for humanity an abundance of divine gifts. However, he also knows that, in order worthily to pronounce the words of consecration in the name of Christ— "This is my Body", "This is the cup of my Blood"—he must be profoundly united to Christ and seek to reproduce Christ's countenance in himself. The more intensely he lives in Christ, the more authentically he can celebrate the Eucharist.

The Second Vatican Council recalled that "especially in the sacrifice of the Mass (priests) act in a special way in the person of Christ"[2] and that without a priest there can be no Eucharist sacrifice; however, it emphasized that those who celebrate this sacrifice must fulfil their role in intimate spiritual union with Christ, with great humility, as his ministers in the service of the community. They must "imitate what they handle, so that as they celebrate the mystery of the Lord's death they may take care to mortify their members from vice and concupiscence."[3]

In offering the Eucharistic sacrifice, presbyters must offer themselves personally with Christ, accepting all the renunciation and sacrifice required by their priestly life. Again and always, *with* Christ and *like* Christ, *Sacerdos et Hostia*.

3. If the priest "hears" this truth proposed to him and to all the faithful as the voice of the New Testament and Tradition, he will grasp the Council's earnest recommendation of the "daily celebration (of the Eucharist), which is an act of Christ and the Church even if it is impossible for the faithful to be present."[4] The tendency to celebrate the Eucharist only when there was an assembly of the faithful emerged in those years.

According to the Council, although everything possible should be done to gather the faithful for the celebration, it is also true that, even if the priest is alone, the Eucharistic offering which he performs in the name of Christ has the effectiveness that comes from Christ and always obtains new graces for the Church. Therefore I, too, recommend to priests and to all the Christian people that they ask the Lord for a stronger faith in this value of the Eucharist.

## Strengthened by Visits to the Blessed Sacrament

4. The 1971 Synod of Bishops took up the conciliar doctrine, declaring: "Even if the Eucharist should be celebrated without participation of the faithful, it nevertheless remains the center of the life of the entire Church and the heart of priestly existence."[5]

This is a wonderful expression: "The center of the life of the entire Church." *The Eucharist makes the Church, just as the Church makes the Eucharist.* The presbyter, having been given the charge of building up the Church, performs this task essentially through the Eucharist. Even when the participation of the faithful is lacking, he cooperates in gathering people around Christ in the Church by offering the Eucharist.

The Synod speaks further of the Eucharist as the "heart of priestly existence." This means that the presbyter, desiring to be and remain personally and profoundly attached to Christ, finds him first in the Eucharist, the sacrament which brings about this intimate union, open to a growth which can reach the heights of mystical identification.

5. At this level, too, which is that of so many holy priests, the priestly soul is not closed in on itself, because in a particular way in the Eucharist it draws on the "charity of him who gives himself as food to the faithful."[6] Thus he feels led to give himself to the faithful to whom he distributes the Body of Christ. It is precisely in being nourished by this Body that he is impelled to help the faithful to open themselves in turn to that same presence, drawing nourishment from his infinite charity, in order to draw ever richer fruit from the sacrament.

To this end the presbyter can and must provide the atmosphere necessary for a worthy Eucharistic celebration. It is the atmosphere of prayer: liturgical prayer, to which the people must be called and trained; the prayer of personal contemplation; the prayer of sound Christian popular tradition, which can prepare for, follow and to some extent also accompany the Mass; the prayer of holy places, of sacred art, of sacred song, of sacred music, (especially on the organ), which is incarnated as it were in the formulas and rites, and continually inspires and uplifts everything so that it can participate in giving praise to God and in the spiritual uplifting of the Christian people gathered in the Eucharist assembly.

6. To priests the Council also recommends, in addition to the daily celebration of the Mass, "personal devotion" to the Holy Eucharist, and particularly that "daily talk with Christ the Lord in their visit to the Blessed Sacrament."[7] Faith in and love for the Eucharist cannot allow Christ's

presence in the tabernacle to remain alone.[8] Already in the Old Testament we read that God dwelt in a "tent" (or "tabernacle"), which was called the "meeting tent".[9] The meeting was desired by God. It can be said that in the tabernacle of the Eucharist too Christ is present in view of a dialogue with his new people and with individual believers. The presbyter is the first one called to enter this meeting tent, to visit Christ in the tabernacle for a "daily talk".

Lastly, I want to recall that, more than any other, the presbyter is called to share the fundamental disposition of Christ in this sacrament, that is, the "thanksgiving" from which it takes its name. Uniting himself with Christ the Priest and Victim, the presbyter shares not only his offering, but also his feelings, his disposition of gratitude to the Father for the benefits he has given to humanity, to every soul, to the priest himself, to all those who in heaven and on earth have been allowed to share in the glory of God. *Gratias agimus tibi propter magnam gloriam tuam. . . .*

Thus, to counter the expressions of accusation and protest against God—which are often heard in the world—the priest offers the chorus of praise and blessing, which is raised up by those who are able to recognize in man and in the world the signs of an infinite goodness.

## NOTES

1. Cf. D-S, 1764
2. *Presbyterorum ordinis*, n. 13
3. *Ibid.*, n. 13
4. *Ibid.*, n. 13
5. Cf. *Enchiridion Vaticanum*, 4, 1201
6. *Presbyterorum ordinis*, n. 13
7. *Presbyterorum ordinis*, n. 18
8. CCC, n. 1418
9. Ex 33:7

# IX

# Priests: Specially Linked to the Blessed Virgin Mary

General Audience of Wednesday June 30, 1993

*As Mary first shared spiritually in her Son's sacrifice, she can obtain for his ministers the graces they need to respond fully to their vocation.*

1. The biographies of saintly priests always document the great role they attributed in their spiritual life to Mary. To the "written lives" corresponds the experience of the "lived lives" of so many dear, venerable priests whom the Lord appointed as true ministers of divine grace among the peoples entrusted to their pastoral care or as preachers, chaplains, confessors, professors, writers. Spiritual directors and masters insist on the importance of devotion to our Lady in the priest's life, as an effective support on the path of sanctification, a constant comfort during personal trials and a powerful strength in the apostolate.

The 1971 Synod of Bishops too passed on these expressions of Christian tradition to priests today when it recommended: "With his mind raised to heaven and sharing in the communion of saints, the priest should very often turn

to Mary, the Mother of God, who received the Word of God
with perfect faith, and daily ask her for the grace of conforming himself to her Son."[1] The profound reason for the
presbyter's devotion to Mary most holy is based on the
essential relationship established in the divine plan between the Mother of Jesus and the priesthood of her Son's
ministers. We want to reflect on this important aspect of
priestly spirituality and draw practical conclusions from it.

2. Mary's relationship to the priesthood derives primarily
from the fact of her motherhood. Becoming the Mother of
Christ by her consent to the angel's message, Mary became
the Mother of the High Priest. This is an objective reality:
by assuming a human nature in the incarnation, the eternal
Son of God fulfilled the necessary condition for becoming
the one Priest of humanity through his death and resurrection.[2] We can marvel at the perfect correspondence between
Mary and her Son at the moment of the incarnation.

Indeed, the Letter to the Hebrews reveals to us that when
he "came into the world," Jesus gave a priestly orientation
to his personal sacrifice and said to God: "Sacrifice and
offering to you did not desire, but a body you prepared for
me; . . . Then I said, 'Behold, I come to do your will, O
God'."[3] The Gospel tells us that at the same moment the
Virgin Mary expressed the same attitude, saying: "Behold,
I am handmaid of the Lord. May it be done to me according
to your word."[4]

### Following Mary: Fully Cooperating
### in Christ's Priestly Mission

This perfect correspondence shows us that a close relationship has been established between Mary's motherhood and
Christ's priesthood. By that very fact a special bond exists
between the priestly ministry and Mary most holy.

3. As you know, the Blessed Virgin fulfilled her role as mother
not only in physically begetting Jesus but also in his moral
formation. In virtue of her motherhood, she was respon-

sible for raising the child Jesus in a way appropriate to his priestly mission, the meaning of which she learned from the message of the incarnation.

In Mary's consent we can recognize an assent to the substantial truth of Christ's priesthood and the willingness to cooperate in fulfilling it in the world. This lays the objective basis for the role Mary was called to play too in the formation of Christ's ministers, sharers in his priesthood. I called attention to this in the Post-Synodal Apostolic Exhortation *Pastores dabo vobis* every aspect of priestly formation can be referred to Mary.[5]

4. We know further that our Lady fully lived *the mystery* of Christ, which she discovered ever more deeply through her personal reflection on the events of her Son's birth and childhood.[6] With mind and heart she strove to fathom the divine plan in order consciously and effectively to cooperate in it. Who today better than she could enlighten the ministers of her Son, leading them to fathom the "unspeakable riches" of his mystery in order to act in conformity with his priestly mission?

Mary was uniquely associated with Christ's priestly sacrifice, sharing his will to save the world by the cross. She was the first to share spiritually in his offering as *Sacerdos et Hostia,* and did so most perfectly. As such, she can obtain and give grace to those who share in her Son's priesthood on the ministerial level, the grace moving them to respond ever more fully to the demands of spiritual oblation that the priesthood entails: in particular, the grace of faith, hope and perseverance in trials, recognized as a challenge to share more generously in the redemptive sacrifice.

## Entrusted by Our Lord to the Motherly Care of the Virgin Mary

5. On Calvary Jesus entrusted a new motherhood to Mary when he said to her: "Woman, behold your son!"[7] We cannot overlook the fact that at the time this motherhood was

proclaimed in regard to a "priest", the beloved disciple. In fact, according to the synoptic Gospels John too received from the Master at the Supper on the previous night to the power to renew the sacrifice of the cross in his memory; with the other Apostles he belonged to the group of the first "priests"; now at Mary's side he replaced the one, supreme Priest who was leaving the world.

Certainly, Jesus' intention at that moment was to establish Mary's universal motherhood in the life of grace for every disciple at the time and for all ages. But we cannot ignore the fact that this motherhood took on a concrete, immediate form in relation to an "Apostle-priest." And we can think that Jesus' gaze extended beyond John to the long series of his "priests" in every age until the end of the world. For them in particular, taken one by one, like the beloved disciple, he made that entrustment to Mary's motherhood.

Jesus also said to John: "Behold, your mother!"[8] To the beloved disciple he entrusted the task of caring for Mary as his own mother, of loving her, venerating her and protecting her for the remaining years of her life on earth, but in the light of what was written for her in heaven, where she would be assumed and glorified. These words are the origin of Marian devotion: the fact that they were addressed to a "priest" is significant. Can we not then draw the conclusion that the "priest" is charged with promoting and developing this devotion? That he is the one primarily responsible for it?

### Always Confident of the Help of the Blessed Virgin Mary

In his Gospel John thought it important to stress that "from that hour the disciple took her into his home."[9] Thus he responded immediately to Christ's invitation and took Mary with him with a reverence appropriate to the circumstances. I would like to say that in this respect too he appeared a "true priest": certainly a faithful disciple of Jesus.

For every priest, taking Mary into his own home means finding a place for her in his own life, remaining in habitual union with her in his thoughts, feelings, zeal for the kingdom of God and for devotion to her.[10]

6. What should we *ask* of Mary as "Mother of priests"? Today, as and perhaps more than at any other time, the priest must ask Mary particularly for the grace of knowing how to accept God's gift with grateful love, fully appreciating it as she did in the *Magnificat*; the grace of generosity in self-giving, in order to imitate her example as a "generous Mother", the grace of purity and fidelity in the obligation of celibacy, following her example as the "faithful Virgin"; the grace of a burning, merciful love, in the light of her witness as the "Mother of mercy."

The presbyter must always remember that in the difficulties he will meet he can count on Mary's help. In her and to her he confides and entrusts himself and his pastoral ministry, asking her to make it yield abundant fruit. Finally, he looks to her as the perfect model of his life and ministry, because she is the one, as the Council says, who "under the guidance of the Holy Spirit made a total dedication of herself for the mystery of human redemption. Priests should always venerate and love her, with a filial devotion and worship, as the Mother of the supreme and eternal Priest, as Queen of Apostles, and as protectress of their ministry."[11]

I urge my brothers in the priesthood increasingly to nourish this "true devotion to Mary" and to draw its practical consequences far their life and ministry. I urge all the faithful to join us priests in entrusting themselves to our Lady and in invoking her graces for themselves and for the whole Church.

# NOTES

1. *Enchiridion Vaticanum*, IV, 1202
2. Cf. Heb 5:1
3. Heb 10:5-7
4. Lk 1:38
5. *Pastores dabo vobis* n. 82
6. Cf. Lk 2:19, 2:51
7. Jn 19:26
8. Jn 19:27
9. Jn 19:27
10. Cf. CCC, nn. 2673-2679
11. *Presbyterorum ordinis*, n. 18

# X

# Priests: Called to be Men of Charity

General Audience of Wednesday July 7, 1993

*Those to whom the Lord gives the mission of being shepherds through priestly ordination are called to embody the heroic love of Jesus himself.*

1. In the preceding catecheses devoted to presbyters we have already mentioned several times the importance of fraternal charity in their lives. Now we want to discuss this more explicitly, beginning with the very root of this charity in the priest's life. This root is found in his identity as a "man of God." The First Letter of John teaches us that "God is love."[1] Since he is a "man of God" the priest must be a man of charity. He would have no true love for God (nor even true piety or true apostolic zeal) without love for his neighbor.

Jesus himself showed the connection between love for God and love for neighbor, since "loving the Lord, your God, with all your heart" cannot be separated from "loving your neighbor."[2] Consistently, therefore, the author of the Letter cited above reasons: "This is the commandment we have from him: whoever loves God must also love his brother."[3]

2. Speaking of himself, Jesus describes this love as that of a "good shepherd" who does not seek his own interest, his

own advantage, like a hired hand. He notes that the Good Shepherd loves his sheep to the point of giving his own life.[4] Thus it is a love to the point of heroism.

We know to what extent this was realized in the life and death of Jesus. Those who, in virtue of priestly ordination, receive the mission of shepherds are called to present anew in their lives and witness to with their actions the heroic love of the Good Shepherd.

3. In Jesus' life one can clearly see the essential features of the "pastoral charity" that he had for his brothers and sisters, "men", and that he asks his brother "shepherds" to imitate. Above all, his love was humble: "I am meek and humble of heart."[5] Significantly, he urges his Apostles to renounce their personal ambitions and any spirit of domination so as to imitate the example of the "Son of Man" who "did not come to be served but to serve and to give his life as a ransom for many."[6]

As a result the mission of shepherd cannot be carried out with a superior or authoritarian attitude,[7] which would irritate the faithful and perhaps drive them from the fold. In the footsteps of Christ the Good Shepherd we must be formed in a spirit of humble service.[8]

Jesus also gives the example of a love filled with compassion, i.e., a sincere, active sharing in the sufferings and problems of the faithful. He feels compassion for the crowd without a shepherd;[9] for this reason he is concerned to guide them by his words of life and begins to "teach them many things."[10]

With this same compassion he healed many of the sick,[11] as a sign of his intention to give spiritual healing; he multiplies the loaves for the hungry,[12] an eloquent symbol of the Eucharist; he is moved by the sight of human misery,[13] and wants to bring healing; he shared the pain of those who mourn the loss of a dear relative;[14] he shows mercy even to sinners,[15] in union with the Father who is full of compassion for the prodigal son[16] and prefers mercy to ritual sacrifice;[17] and there are cases in which he rebukes his adversaries for not understanding his mercy.[18]

4. In this regard it is significant that the Letter to the Hebrews, in the light of Jesus' life and death, again sees an essential feature of the authentic priesthood in solidarity and compassion. Indeed, it reaffirms that the High Priest, "taken from among men and made their representative before God, . . . is able to deal patiently with the ignorant and erring."[19] Therefore, the eternal Son of God too "had to become like his brothers in every way, that he might be a *merciful* and *faithful High Priest* before God to expiate the sins of the people."[20] As a result our great consolation as Christians is knowing that "we do not have a High Priest who is unable to sympathize with our weaknesses, but one who has similarly been tested in every way, yet without sin."[21]

The presbyter thus finds in Christ the model of a true love for the suffering, the poor, the afflicted and especially for sinners, because Jesus is close to human beings with a life like our own; he endured trials and tribulations like our own; therefore he is full of compassion for us and "is able to deal patiently with erring sinners."[22] Finally, he is able effectively to help those sorely tried: "Since he was himself tested through what he suffered he is able to help those who are tempted."[23]

## Images of the Love of the Good Shepherd

5. Continuing in this light of divine love, the Second Vatican Council presents priestly consecration as a source of pastoral charity: "The priests of the New Testament are, it is true, by their vocation to ordination, set apart in some way in the midst of the People of God, but this is not in order that they should be separated from that people or from anyone, but that they should be completely consecrated to the task for which God chooses them. They could not be the servants of Christ unless they were witnesses and dispensers of a life other than that of this earth.

"On the other hand they would be powerless to serve men if they remained aloof from their life and circumstances."[24] At issue are two demands on which the two aspects of priestly behavior are based: for presbyters, "their very ministry makes a special claim on them not to conform themselves to this world; still it requires at the same time that they should live among men in this world and that as good shepherds they should know their sheep and should also seek to lead back those who do not belong to this fold, so that they too may hear the voice of Christ and there may be one fold and one Shepherd."[25] This explains Paul's intense activity in collecting aid for the poorest communities,[26] and the recommendation made by the author of the Letter to the Hebrews to practice a sharing of possessions *(koinonía)* in supporting one another as true followers of Christ.[27]

6. According to the Council, the presbyter who wants to be conformed to the Good Shepherd and reproduce in himself his charity for his brothers and sisters will have to be committed to some very important tasks today, even more so than in other times: to know his own sheep,[28] especially by contacts, visits, relations of friendship, planned or occasional meetings, etc., always for a reason and with the spirit of a good shepherd; to welcome, as Jesus did, the people who come to him, remaining ready and able to listen, wanting to understand, open and genuinely kind, engaging in deeds and activities to aid the poor and unfortunate, to cultivate and practice those "virtues which are rightly held in high esteem in human relations.

Such qualities are goodness of heart, sincerity, strength and constancy of mind, careful attention to justice, courtesy, etc.,"[29] as well as patience, readiness to forgive quickly and generously, kindness, affability, the capacity to be obliging and helpful without playing the benefactor. There are a myriad of human and pastoral virtues which the fragrance of Christ's charity can and must determine in the priest's conduct.[30]

## All Priestly Activities Rooted in the Eucharist

7. Sustained by charity, the presbyter can, in the exercise of his ministry, follow the example of Christ, whose food was to do his Father's will. In loving submission to this will the priest will find the principle and source of unity in his life. The Council states that priests can achieve this unity "by joining themselves with Christ in the recognition of the Father's will. . . . In this way, by adopting the role of the Good Shepherd they will find in the practice of pastoral charity itself the bond of priestly perfection which will achieve unity in their life and activity."[31] The source on which to draw this charity is always the Eucharist, which is "the center and root of the priest's whole life"; therefore, his soul must strive "to make his own what is enacted on the altar of sacrifice."[32]

The grace and charity of the altar thus spreads to the pulpit, the confessional, the parish office, the school, recreational activities, homes and streets, hospitals public transportation and the communication media, wherever the priest has the opportunity to carry out his task as a shepherd: in every case it is his Mass which is spread; it is his spiritual union with Christ the Priest and Victim that leads him to be, as Ignatius of Antioch said, "God's wheat in order to become pure bread" for the good of his brothers and sisters.[33]

# NOTES

1. St. Paul's Letter to John 4:8
2. Cf. Mt 22:36-40
3. 1 Jn 4:21
4. Cf. Jn 10:11, 15
5. Mt 11:29
6. Mk 10:45; Mt 20:28; cf. *Pastores dabo vobis*, nn. 21-22
7. Cf. 1 Pt 5:3

8. Cf. *CCC*, n. 876
9. Cf. Mt 9:36
10. Mk 6:34
11. Mt 14:14
12. Mt 15:32, Mk 8:2
13. Mt 20:34; Mk 1:41
14. Lk 7:13; Jn 11:33-35
15. Cf. Lk 15:1-2
16. Cf. Lk 15:20
17. Cf. Mt 9:10-13
18. Mt 12:7
19. Heb 5:1-2
20. *Ibid.*, 2:17
21. *Ibid.*, 4:15
22. Heb 5:2
23. *Ibid.*, 2:18
24. *Presbyterorum ordinis*, n. 3
25. *Ibid.*
26. Cf. 1 Cor 16:1-4
27. Cf. Heb 13:16
28. *Presbyterorum ordinis* n. 3
29. *Ibid.*
30. Cf. *Pastores dabo vobis*, n. 23
31. *Presbyterorum ordinis*, n. 14
32. *Ibid.*
33. Cf. *Epist. ad Romanos*

# XI

# Priests: Consecrated to Christ through Celibacy

General Audience of Saturday July 17, 1993

*In the life of celibacy the Church sees a sign of the priest's special consecration to Christ as one who has left everything to follow him.*

1. In the Gospels when Jesus called his first Apostles to make them "fishers of men,"[1] they "left *everything* and followed him."[2] One day it was Peter who remembered this aspect of the apostolic vocation and said to Jesus: "We have given up everything and followed you."[3] Jesus then listed all the necessary detachments "for my sake", he said "and for the sake of the Gospel."[4] This did not only mean renouncing material possessions, such as "house" or "lands", but also being separated from loved ones: "brothers or sisters or mother or father or children"—according to Matthew and Mark—"wife or brothers or parents or children"—according to Luke.[5]

Here we note the difference in vocations. Jesus did not demand this radical renunciation of family life from all his disciples, although he did require the first place in their hearts, when he said: "Whoever loves father or mother more than me is not worthy of me, and whoever loves son or daughter more than me is not worthy of me."[6] The demand for practical renunciation is proper to the apostolic life or the life of special consecration. Called by Jesus, "James, the son of Zebedee, and his brother John" left not only the boat on which they were "mending their nets", but also their father who was with them.[7]

These observations help us understand the reason for the Church's legislation on *priestly celibacy*. In fact, the Church has considered and still considers that it belongs to the logic of priestly consecration and to the total belonging to Christ resulting from it, in order consciously to fulfill his mandate of evangelization and the spiritual life.

### Single-heartedly Focused on the Gospel

2. Indeed, in the Gospel according to Matthew, shortly before the passage cited above about leaving loved ones, Jesus expresses in strong Semitic language another renunciation required "for the sake of the Gospel", that is, the renunciation of marriage. "Some have made themselves eunuchs for the sake of the kingdom of heaven."[8] They are committed to celibacy, that is, in order to put themselves entirely at the service of the "Gospel of the kingdom."[9]

In his First Letter to the Corinthians, the Apostle Paul states that he had resolved to take this path and shows the coherence of his own decision, declaring: "An unmarried man is anxious about the things of the Lord, how he may please the Lord. But a married man is anxious about the things of the world, how he may please his wife, and he is divided!"[10] It is certainly inappropriate for someone to be "divided", someone who, like the priest, has been called to be concerned about the things of the Lord. As the Council says, the commitment of celibacy, stemming from a tradition linked to Christ, has "been highly esteemed as a feature of priestly life. For it is at once a sign of pastoral charity and an incentive to it, as well as being in a special way a source of spiritual fruitfulness in the world."[11]

It is quite true that in the Eastern Churches many presbyters are legitimately married in accordance with their own canon law. Even in those Churches, however, bishops are celibate, as are a number of priests. The difference in discipline, related to conditions of time and place evaluated by the Church, is explained by the fact that perfect continence, as the Council says, "is not demanded of the priesthood by its nature."[12] It does not belong to the essence of the priesthood as Holy Orders, and thus is not imposed in an absolute way in all the Churches. Nevertheless, there is no doubt about its *suitability* and indeed its *appropriateness* to the demands of *Sacred Orders*. As was said, it belongs to the *logic* of *consecration*.

3. Jesus is the concrete ideal of this form of consecrated life, an example for everyone, but especially for priests. He lived as a celibate, and for this reason he was able to devote all his energy to preaching the kingdom of God and to serving people, with a heart open to all humanity, as the founder of a new spiritual family. His choice was truly "for the sake of the kingdom of heaven."[13]

By his example Jesus gave an orientation that was followed. According to the Gospels, it appears that the Twelve, destined to be the first to share in his priesthood, renounced family life in order to follow him. The Gospels never speak of wives or children in regard to the Twelve, although they tell us that Peter was a married man before he was called by Jesus.[14]

## Celibacy Reflects the Mystical Marriage of Christ and the Church

4. Jesus did not promulgate a *law*, but proposed the *ideal* of celibacy for the new priesthood he was instituting. This ideal was increasingly asserted in the Church. One can understand that in the first phase of Christianity's spread and development a large number of priests were married men, chosen and ordained in the wake of Jewish tradition. We know that in the Letters to Timothy[15] and to Titus,[16] one

of the qualities required of the men chosen as presbyters is that they be good fathers of families, married only once (i.e.: faithful to their wives). This is a phase in the Church's process of being organized, and, one could say, of testing which discipline of the states of life best corresponds to the ideal and the "counsels" taught by the Lord.

On the basis of experience and reflection the discipline of celibacy gradually spread to the point of becoming the general practice in the Western Church as a result of canonical legislation. It was not merely the consequence of a juridical and disciplinary fact: it was the growth of the Church's realization of the appropriateness of priestly celibacy not only for historical and practical reasons, but also for those arising from an ever better awareness of the congruence of celibacy and the demands of the priesthood.

5. The Second Vatican Council gave the reasons for this "inner consonance" of celibacy and the priesthood: "By preserving virginity or celibacy for the sake of the kingdom of heaven priests are consecrated in a new and excellent way to Christ. They more readily cling to him with undivided heart and dedicate themselves more freely in him and through him to the service of God and men. They are less encumbered in their service of his kingdom and of the task of heavenly regeneration. In this way they become better fitted for a broader acceptance of fatherhood in Christ." They "recall that mystical marriage, established by God and destined to be fully revealed in the future, by which the Church holds Christ as her only Spouse. Moreover they are made a living sign of that world to come in which the children of the resurrection shall neither be married or take wives."[17]

These lofty, noble spiritual reasons can be summarized in the following essential points: a more complete adherence to Christ, loved and served with an undivided heart;[18] greater availability to serve Christ's kingdom and to carry out their own tasks in the Church the most exclusive choice of a spiritual fruitfulness;[19] leading a life more like that definitive one in the world to come, and therefore, more exemplary for life here below.

This is a valid reason for all times, including our own, and the supreme criterion of every judgement and every choice in harmony with the invitation to "leave everything" made by Jesus to the disciples and particularly to the Apostles. For this reason the 1971 Synod of Bishops confirmed: "The law of priestly celibacy existing in the Latin Church is to be kept in its entirety."[20]

**Gifted by the Father**

6. It is true that today the practice of celibacy faces obstacles, sometimes grave ones, in the subjective and objective conditions in which priests happen to live. The Synod of Bishops considered them, but held that even today's difficulties can be overcome, if "suitable conditions are fostered, namely: growth of the interior life through prayer, renunciation and fervent love for God and one's neighbor and by other aids to the spiritual life; human balance through well-ordered integration into the fabric of social relationships, fraternal association and companionship with other priests and with the Bishop, through pastoral structures better suited to this purpose and with the assistance also of the community of the faithful."[21]

This is a kind of challenge that the Church makes to the mentality, tendencies and charms of the world, with an ever new desire for consistency with and fidelity to the Gospel ideal. Therefore, although the Supreme Pontiff can consider and decide what is to be done in certain cases, the Synod reaffirmed that in the Latin Church "the priestly ordination of married men is not permitted, even in particular cases."[22] The Church holds that the awareness of total consecration, developed over centuries continues to hold good and to be increasingly improved.

The Church also knows and she reminds presbyters and all the faithful with the Council that "the gift of celibacy, so appropriate to the priesthood of the New Testament, is liberally granted by the Father, provided that those who share Christ's priesthood through the sacrament of Orders, and indeed the whole Church, ask for that gift humbly and earnestly."[23]

Perhaps, however, and even first, it is necessary to ask for the grace of understanding priestly celibacy, which doubtless includes a certain mystery: that of asking for boldness and trust in the absolute attachment to the person and redeeming work of Christ, with a radical renunciation that can seem confusing to human eyes. Jesus himself, in suggesting it, observed that not everyone can understand it.[24] Blessed are they who receive the grace to understand it and remain faithful on this journey!

## NOTES

1. Mt 4:19; Mk 1:17; cf. Lk 5:10
2. Lk 5:11; cf. Mt 4:20, 22; Mk 1:18, 20
3. Mt 19:27; Mk 10:28; cf. Lk 18:28
4. Mk 10:29
5. Lk 18:29
6. Mt 10:37
7. Mt 4:22; cf. Mk 1:20
8. Mt 19:12
9. Cf. Mt 4:23; 9:35; 24:34
10. 1 Cor 7:32-34
11. *Presbyterorum ordinis*, n. 16
12. *Ibid.*
13. Cf. Mt 19:12
14. Cf. Mt 8:14; Mk 1:30; Lk 4:38
15. 1 Tm 3:2-3
16. Titus 1:6
17. *Presbyterorum ordinis*, n. 16; cf. *Pastores dabo vobis*, nn. 29, 50; CCC, n. 1579
18. Cf. 1 Cor 7:32-33
19. Cf. 1 Cor 4:15
20. *Enchiridion Vaticanum*, IV, 1219
21. *Ibid.*, IV, 1216
22. *Ibid.*, IV, 1220
23. *Presbyterorum ordinis*, n. 16
24. Cf. Mt 19:10-12

# XII

# Priests: Following Christ as Model of Priestly Poverty and Detachment

General Audience of Wednesday July 21, 1993

*As all Christ's followers, priests must cultivate an interior detachment from earthly goods and a generous openness to the needs of others.*

1. One of the renunciations requested by Jesus of his disciples is that of earthly goods, particularly wealth.[1] It is a request directed to all Christians in regard to the *spirit of poverty,* that is, the interior detachment from earthly goods which makes them generous in sharing these goods with others. Poverty is required of a life inspired by faith in Christ and by love for him. It is a *spirit* that also demands a *practice,* with each one's renunciation of these goods corresponding to his condition both in civil life and his state in the Church by virtue of the Christian vocation, both as an individual and as a determinate group of people. The spirit of poverty is valid for all; a certain practice of it in conformity with the Gospel is necessary for everyone.

2. The poverty Jesus requested of the Apostles is a current of spirituality that could not end with them or be reduced to particular groups: the spirit of poverty is necessary for everyone in every time and place; its lack would be a betrayal of the Gospel. Faithfulness to the *spirit*, however, does not require of Christians in general or of priests the *practice* of a radical poverty with the renunciation of all property or even the abolition of this human right. The Church's Magisterium has frequently condemned those who claimed this was necessary;[2] she has sought to lead thought and practice on a course of moderation.

It is comforting to note, however, that over the course of time and under the influence of ancient and modern saints, the clergy has acquired an increasing awareness of a call to Gospel poverty, both as a spirit and as a practice corresponding to the demands of priestly consecration. The social and economic situation in which the clergy of almost all the countries of the world live has helped to concretize the condition of real poverty for individuals and institutions, even when the latter by their very nature need many means to carry out their work. In many cases it is a difficult and distressing condition, which the Church strives to overcome in various ways, mainly by appealing to the charity of the faithful to receive their necessary contribution in order to provide for worship, works of charity, support for the pastors of souls and for missionary projects.

However, achieving a new sense of poverty is a blessing for priestly life, as for that of all Christians, because it allows them to conform themselves better to Jesus' counsels and suggestions.

### In the World but Not of It

3. Gospel poverty—it should be made clear—entails no disdain for earthly goods, which God has put at man's disposal for his life and his cooperation in the plan of creation. According to the Second Vatican Council, the presbyter,

like every other Christian, having a mission of praise and thanksgiving, must acknowledge and glorify the generosity of the heavenly Father who is revealed in created goods.[3]

Nevertheless, the Council goes on to say that priests, although living in the midst of the world, must always keep in mind that, as the Lord said, they do not belong to the world,[4] and therefore, they must be freed from every disordered attachment in order to obtain "that spiritual insight through which is found a right attitude to the world and to earthly goods."[5] It must be recognized that this is a delicate problem.

On the one hand, "the Church's mission is carried out in the midst of the world and created goods are absolutely necessary for man's personal progress." Jesus did not forbid his Apostles from accepting the goods necessary for their earthly life. Rather he asserted their right in this matter when he said in a discourse on mission: "Eat and drink what is offered to you, for the laborer deserves his payment."[6]

St. Paul reminds the Corinthians that "the Lord ordered that those who preach the Gospel should live by the Gospel."[7] He himself insisted on the rule that "one who is being instructed in the word should share all good things with his instructor."[8] It is right then that presbyters have earthly goods and use them "for those purposes to which the teaching of Christ and the direction of the Church allow them to be devoted."[9] The Council did not fail to give practical directions in this regard.

Above all, the management of ecclesiastical property, properly so called, must be guaranteed "according to the norm of ecclesiastical laws and with the help, as far as possible, of skilled lay people." This property is always to be used for "the organization of divine worship, the provision of decent support for the clergy, and the exercise of works of the apostolate and of charity, especially for the benefit of those in need."[10]

The goods acquired by the exercise of any ecclesiastical office must be used primarily "for their own decent support and the fulfillment of the duties of their state. They should be willing to devote whatever is left over to the good of the Church or to works of charity." This must be particularly stressed: neither for priests nor for bishops can ecclesiastical office be an occasion of personal enrichment or of profit for their own family. "Hence priests, far from setting their hearts on riches must always avoid all avarice and carefully refrain from all appearance of trafficking."[11] In any case, it must be kept in mind that all possessions must be used in the light of the Gospel.

4. The same must be said about the priest's involvement in secular activities or those pertaining to the management of earthly affairs outside of a religious, sacred context. The 1971 Synod of Bishops stated that "as a general rule, the priestly ministry shall be a full-time occupation. Sharing in the secular activities of men is by no means to be considered the principal end nor can such participation suffice to give expression to the priests' specific responsibility."[12] This was a stance taken in response to a tendency appearing here and there toward the secularization of the priest's activity in the sense that he could be involved, as are lay people, in exercising a trade or secular profession.

### Like the Good Shepherd

In truth there are circumstances in which the only effective way for the Church to re-establish links with a workplace that ignores Christ can be the presence of priests who exercise a trade in that environment, e.g., by becoming workers with the workers. The generosity of these priests deserves to be praised. It should be noted, however, that by taking on secular lay tasks and positions the priest runs the risk of reducing his own sacred ministry to a secondary role or even of eliminating it.

Because of this risk, confirmed by experience, the Council had already stressed the need of approval by the competent authority for engaging in manual labor and sharing the living conditions of workers.[13] The Synod gave as a practical rule the appropriateness, or less, of a certain secular occupation with the purposes of the priesthood; "this is to be judged by the local bishop with his presbyterate, and if necessary in with his presbyterate, and if necessary in consultation with the Episcopal Conference."[14]

On the other hand, clearly there are special cases today, as in the past, in which some particularly talented and well-trained presbyters can be involved in labor and cultural activities that are not directly Church-related. However, care must be taken so that these cases remain exceptional. Even then the criterion determined by the Synod must always be applied, in order to be faithful to the Gospel and the Church.

5. We shall conclude this catechesis by turning once again to the figure of Jesus Christ, the High Priest, the Good Shepherd and supreme model for priests. He is the presbyter's example of being stripped of one's earthly goods, if he wants to be conformed to the demand of evangelical poverty. Jesus was indeed born in poverty and he lived in it. St. Paul admonished: "He made himself poor though he was rich."[15] To someone who wanted to follow him, Jesus said of himself: "The foxes have lairs, the birds of the sky have nests, but the Son of Man has nowhere to lay his head."[16] These words show a complete detachment from all earthly comforts. However, one should not conclude that Jesus lived in destitution. Other Gospel passages state that he received and accepted invitations to the homes of rich people,[17] he had women who helped support him in his financial needs,[18] and he was able to give alms to the poor.[19] Nevertheless, there is no doubt about the spirit and life of poverty that distinguished him.

## Open to the Poor

The same spirit of poverty should inspire the priest's behavior, characterizing his attitude, life and very image as a pastor and man of God. It is expressed in disinterest and detachment towards money, in renunciation of all greed for possessing earthly goods, in a simple lifestyle, in the choice of a modest dwelling accessible to all, in rejecting everything that is or appears to be luxurious, while striving to give himself more and more freely to the service of God and the faithful.

6. Finally, let us add that, having been called by Jesus to "preach Good News to the poor" and in accordance with his example, "priests and bishops alike are to avoid everything that might in any way antagonize the poor."[20] Instead, by fostering in themselves the Gospel spirit of poverty, they will be in a position to show their own preferential option for the poor, translating it into sharing, into personal and community works of assistance, including material aid, to the needy. It is a witness to the Poor Christ, which is given today by so many priests, poor themselves and the friends of the poor. It is a great flame of love enkindled in the life of the clergy and the Church. If occasionally in the past the clergy could in some places appear among the ranks of the wealthy, today they feel honored, with the whole Church, in being found in the first row among the "new poor." This is great progress in following Christ on the path of the Gospel.

## NOTES

1. Cf. Mt 19:21; Mk 10:21, Lk 12:33, 18:22
2. Cf. DS 760, 930f, 1097
3. *Presbyterorum Ordinis*, n. 17
4. Cf. Jn 17:14-16
5. *Ibid.*; cf. *Pastores dabo vobis*, n. 30
6. Lk 10:7 cf. Mt 10:10
7. 1 Cor 9:14
8. Gal 6:6
9. *Presbyterorum ordinis*, n. 17

10. *Ibid.*
11. *Ibid.*
12. *Enchiridion Vaticanum,* IV, 1191
13. Cf. *Presbyterorum ordinis,* n. 8
14. *Enchiridion Vaticanum,* IV, 1192
15. 2 Cor 8:9
16. Lk 9:58
17. Cf. Mt 9:10- 11, Mk 2:15-16, Lk 5:29-7:36, 19:5-6
18. Lk 8:2-3, cf. Mt 27:55, Mk 15:40, Lk 23:55-56
19. Cf. Jn 13:29
20. *Presbyterorum ordinis,* n. 17

# XIII

# Priests: Without any Political Mission

General Audience of Wednesday July 28, 1993

*By calling for universal love, Christ clearly identified the principles for the right ordering of politics, but he was not involved in worldly affairs.*

1. The discussion of the presbyter's detachment from earthly goods is connected with that of his relationship to *political affairs*. Today more than ever one observes a continual interaction between economics and politics, both in the vast framework of problems on the national level, as well as in the more limited areas of personal and family life. This happens in electing one's own parliamentary representatives and public officials, in supporting the list of candidates presented to the citizens, in the choice of parties, and in statements on individuals, programmes and budgets in regard to the handling of public affairs. It would be a mistake for politics to depend exclusively or primarily on the economic context. However, high-level projects in service to the human person and the common good are influenced by it and cannot fail to take into account questions concerning the possession, use, allocation and distribution of earthly goods.

2. All these points have an ethical aspect that concerns priests too, precisely because of their service to man and society in accordance with the mission they received from Christ. He did teach a doctrine and formulate precepts that shed light not only on the life of individuals but also on that of society. In particular, Jesus formulated the precept of mutual love, which implies respect for every person and his rights; it implies rules of social justice aiming at recognizing what is each person's due and at harmoniously sharing earthly goods among individuals, families and groups.

In addition, Jesus stressed the universal quality of love, above and beyond the differences of race and nationality constituting humanity. It could be said that in calling himself the "Son of Man", he wanted to state, by the very way he presented his messianic identity, that his work was meant for every human person, without discrimination of class, language, culture, or ethnic and social group. Proclaiming peace for his disciples and for all people, Jesus laid the foundation for the precept of fraternal love, solidarity and reciprocal help on a universal scale. For him this clearly was and is the aim and principle of good politics.

### Seeking the Spiritual Liberation of Jesus

Nevertheless, Jesus never wanted to be involved in a political movement and fled from every attempt to draw him into earthly questions and affairs.[1] The kingdom he came to establish does not belong to this world.[2]

For this reason he said to those who wanted him to take a stand regarding the civil power: "Repay to Caesar what belongs to Caesar and to God what belongs to God."[3] He never promised the Jewish nation, to which he belonged and which he loved, the *political* liberation that many expected from the Messiah. Jesus stated that he came as the Son of God to offer humanity, enslaved by sin, *spiritual* liberation and a calling to the kingdom of God;[4] he said that he came not to be served, but to serve;[5] and that his followers too, especially the Apostles, should not think of earthly power and dominion over nations as do the rulers of this world, but be the humble servants of all[6] like their "Teacher and Master."[7]

Certainly, this spiritual liberation brought by Jesus was to have decisive consequences in all areas of social and private life, opening an era of new appreciation for man as a person and for relations between individuals according to justice. However, the Son of Man's immediate concern was not in this direction.

3. It is easy to understand that this state of poverty and freedom is most fitting for the priest, who is the spokesman for Christ in proclaiming human redemption and in his ministry of applying its fruits to every area and at every level of life. As the 1971 Synod of Bishops said: "Together with the entire Church, priests are obliged, to the utmost of their ability, to select a definite pattern of action, when it is a question of the defense of fundamental human rights, the promotion of the full development of persons and the pursuit of the cause of peace and justice; the means must indeed always be consonant with the Gospel. These principles are all valid not only in the individual sphere, but also in the social field; in this regard priests should help the laity to devote themselves to forming their consciences rightly."[8]

## Not Called to Any Partisan Political Activity

This Synod text, which shows that priests are united with all the Church's members in serving justice and peace, allows us to see that the role of priests in social and political action is not identical to that of the laity. This is said more clearly in the *Catechism of the Catholic Church*, where we read: "It is not the responsibility of the Church's pastors to become directly involved in political action and social organization. This task pertains to the vocation of the *lay faithful*, who work on their own initiative together with their fellow citizens."[9]

The lay Christian is called to be directly involved in this activity to make his contribution so that Gospel principles may hold ever greater sway in society. Following Christ, the priest is more directly concerned with the growth of God's kingdom. Like Jesus, he must renounce involvement in political activity, particularly by not taking sides (which almost inevitably happens), in order to remain a man for all in terms of brotherhood and, to the extent that he is accepted as such, of spiritual fatherhood.

Naturally in regard to individuals, groups and situations there can be exceptional cases in which it may seem opportune or even necessary to help or supplement public institutions that are lacking or in disarray, in order to support the cause of justice and peace. Ecclesiastical institutions themselves, even at the highest level, have provided this service in the past, with all the advantages, but also with all the burdens and difficulties that this entails. Providentially, modern political, constitutional and doctrinal development tends in another direction. Civil society has been progressively given institutions and resources to fulfill its own tasks autonomously.[10]

Thus the Church still has her own task: proclaiming the Gospel, limited herself to cooperating in her own way in the common good, without aiming at or accepting a political role.

4. In this light one can better understand what was decided by the 1971 Synod of Bishops regarding the priest's conduct in political life. He certainly retains the right to have personal political opinions and to exercise his right to vote according to his conscience. As the Synod said: "In circumstances in which there legitimately exist different political, social and economic options, priests like all citizens have a right to make their own personal choices. But since political options are by nature contingent and never in an entirely adequate and perennial way interpret the Gospel, the priest, who is the witness of things to come, must keep a certain distance from any political office or involvement."[11]

In particular, he will keep in mind that a political party can never be identified with the truth of the Gospel, and therefore, unlike the Gospel it can never become an object of absolute loyalty. Thus the presbyter will take this relativity into account, even when citizens of the Christian faith laudably form parties explicitly inspired by the Gospel. He must strive to shed the light of Christ on other parties and social groups too.

## Possessed of Neither the Mission nor the Charism of Political Activism

It should be added that the presbyter's right to express his own personal choices is limited by the requirements of his priestly ministry. This limitation too can be an aspect of the poverty he is called to practice on Christ's example. In fact, he can sometimes be obliged to abstain from exercising his own right so that he can be a strong sign of unity, and thus proclaim the Gospel in its fullness. Even more, he must avoid presenting his own choice as the only legitimate one, and within the Christian community, he should respect the maturity of the laity,[12] and even work to help them achieve that maturity by forming their consciences.[13] He will do what is possible to avoid making enemies by taking political stands that cause distrust and drive away the faithful entrusted to his pastoral mission.

5. The 1971 Synod of Bishops especially stressed that the presbyter must abstain from all political activism: "Leadership or active militancy on behalf of any political party is to be excluded by every priest unless, in concrete and exceptional circumstances, this is truly required by the good of the community and receives the consent of the Bishop after consultation with the presbyteral council and, if circumstances call for it, with the Episcopal Conference."[14] Thus it is possible to derogate from the common norm, but this can be justified only in truly exceptional circumstances and requires due authorization.

The Church reminds priests, who in their generous service to the Gospel ideal feel drawn to political involvement in order to help more effectively in reforming political life and in eliminating injustices, exploitation, and every type of oppression, that on this road it is easy to be caught up in partisan strife, with the risk of helping not to bring about the more just world for which they long, but new and worse ways of exploiting poor people. In any case they must know that they have neither the mission nor the charism from above for this political involvement and activism.

**Entrusted with a Pastoral Mission towards Society**

Therefore, I pray and invite you to pray that priests may have ever greater faith in their own pastoral mission for the good of the society in which they live. May they recognize its importance in our age too and understand this statement of the 1971 Synod of Bishops: "The priority of the specific mission which pervades the entire priestly existence must therefore always be kept in mind so that with great confidence, and having a renewed experience of the things of God, priests may be able to announce these things effectively and joyfully to the people who await them."[15]

Yes, I hope and pray that my brother priests today and tomorrow may increasingly be given this gift of spiritual insight, which enables them to understand and to follow the life of poverty taught by Jesus in its political dimension as well.

## NOTES

1. Cf. Jn 6:15
2. Cf. Jn 18:36
3. Mt 22:21
4. Cf. Jn 8:34-36
5. Cf. Mt 20:28

6. Cf. Mt 20:20-28
7. Jn 13:3-14
8. *Enchiridion Vaticanum,* IV, 1194
9. CCC n. 2442
10. Cf. *Gaudium et spes,* nn. 40, 76
11. *Enchiridion Vaticanum,* IV, 1195
12. Cf. *ibid.,* IV, 1196
13. Cf. *ibid.,* IV, 1194
14. *Ibid.,* IV, 1197
15. *Ibid.,* IV, 1198

# XIV

# Priests: Union with Their Bishops and Their Fellow Priests

General Audience of Wednesday August 4, 1993

*A priest's self-denial finds expression in what he does to preserve the communion existing between himself, the Bishop and his fellow priests.*

1. In the previous catecheses we have reflected on the importance which the invitation to, or the evangelical counsels of virginity and poverty have in the priest's life and on how and to what extent they can be practiced in accordance with the spiritual tradition and Christian asceticism, and with the Church's law. Today it is good to recall that Jesus did not hesitate to tell those who wanted to follow him as he carried out his messianic ministry that they had to "deny themselves and take up their cross"[1] to be truly his disciples. This is a great maxim of perfection, valid for the Christian life as the definitive criterion for the heroic virtue of the saints. It applies especially to the priestly life, in which it takes more rigorous forms justified by the particular vocation and special charism of Christ's ministers.

A primary aspect of this "self-denial" appears in the renunciations connected with the commitment to *communion*
that priests are called to fulfill between them and their
Bishop.[2] The institution of the ministerial priesthood took
place within the context of a priestly community and communion. Jesus assembled the first group, that of the Twelve,
and called them to form a union in mutual love. He wanted
to join coworkers to this first "priestly" community. By
sending the 72 disciples on mission, as well as the 12
Apostles, he sent them out two by two,[3] so that they could
help each other in their life and work and develop a habit
of common action in which no one would act alone, independently of the Church community and the community of
the Apostles.

### Renouncing Individualism

2. This fact is confirmed by reflecting on *Christ's call,* which
is the origin of each priest's life and ministry. All priesthood in the Church begins with a vocation. This is addressed to a particular person, but is tied to the calls given
to others within the framework of one and the same plan
for the evangelization and sanctification of the world. Like
the apostles, bishops and priests too are called together,
although in their various personal vocations, by him who
wants to commit them fully to the mystery of redemption.
This community of vocation doubtless implies an openness
of one to the other and of each to all, so as to live and work
in communion.

This does not occur without renouncing an ever real, recur-
ring individualism, without achieving "self-denial"[4] in the
victory of charity over selfishness. The mind of the vocation community, expressed in communion, must nevertheless encourage each and everyone to work
harmoniously, to acknowledge the grace given individually
and collectively to the bishops and presbyters; a grace
granted to each one, not due to personal merits or abilities,

and not only for personal sanctification, but for "building up the Body."[5]

Priestly communion is deeply rooted *in the sacrament of Orders,* in which self-denial becomes an even closer spiritual sharing in the sacrifice of the cross. The sacrament of Orders implies each one's free response to the call addressed to him personally. The response is likewise personal. However, in consecration, the sovereign action of Christ, at work in ordination through the Holy Spirit, creates as it were a new personality, transferring the mentality, conscience and interests of the one receiving the sacrament into the priestly community beyond the sphere of individual aims. It is a psychological fact based on acknowledging the ontological bond between each priest and every other. The priesthood conferred on each one should be exercised in the ontological, psychological and spiritual context of this community. Then there will truly be *priestly communion:* a gift of the Holy Spirit, but also the fruit of a generous response by the priest.

In particular, the grace of Orders creates a special bond between bishops and priests, because priestly ordination is received from the bishop, the priesthood is extended by him and he introduces the newly ordained into the priestly community, of which he himself is a member.

3. Priestly communion presupposes and implies that all, bishops and presbyters, are attached *to the person of Christ.* When Jesus wanted to share his messianic mission with the Twelve, the Gospel of Mark says that he called them and appointed them "as his companions."[6] At the Last Supper he addressed them as those who had stood loyally by him in his trials,[7] urged them to unity and asked the Father for this on their behalf. By remaining united in Christ they would all remain united among themselves.[8]

A vivid awareness of this unity and communion in Christ continued among the Apostles during the preaching that led them from Jerusalem to the various regions of the then

known world under the compelling yet unifying action of
the Spirit of Pentecost. This awareness appears in their
Letters, the Gospels and the Acts.

### Profound Communion with Other Priests

In calling new presbyters to the priesthood, Jesus Christ
also asks them to offer their lives to his own person, thus
intending to unite them to each other by a special relationship of communion with him. This is the true source of the
profound harmony of mind and heart that unites presbyters and bishops in priestly communion.

This communion is fostered by *collaborating in one and the
same work:* spiritually building the community of salvation.
Certainly every priest has his own field of activity to which
he can devote all his abilities and talents, but this field
belongs to the broader work by which every local Church
strives to develop the kingdom of Christ. This work is
essentially communitarian, so that each one must act in
cooperation with the other workers of the same kingdom.

We know how much the desire to work on the same task can
support and spur the common effort of each one. It creates
a feeling of solidarity and makes it possible to accept the
sacrifices that cooperation requires, by respecting others
and welcoming their differences. Henceforth it is important to note that this cooperation is structured around the
relationship between the Bishop and his presbyters; the
subordination of the latter to the former is essential for the
life of the Christian community. Work for the kingdom of
Christ can be carried out and developed only in accordance
with the structure he established.

4. Now I would like to call attention to the role of *the Eucharist* in this communion. At the Last Supper Jesus wanted to
found, in the most complete way, the unity of the apostolic
group, to whom he first entrusted the priestly ministry. In
answer to their dispute about the first place, he gave an
example of humble service by washing their feet.[9] This

settled the conflicts caused by ambition and taught his first priests to seek the last place rather than the first.

During the same Supper Jesus gave his commandment of mutual love[10] and opened the source that would give the strength to observe it: alone the Apostles would not, in fact, have been able to love one another as the Master had loved them; but with *Eucharistic communion* they received the ability to live *ecclesial communion* and, in it, their specific *priestly communion*. By the sacrament Jesus offered them this superior capacity for love and could make a bold supplication to the Father that he accomplished in his disciples a unity like that existing between the Father and the Son.[11]

Finally, at the Last Supper Jesus invests the apostles jointly with their mission and with the power to celebrate the Eucharist in his memory, thus further deepening the bond uniting them. Communion in the power of celebrating the one Eucharist had to be the sign and source of unity for the apostles—and for their successors and coworkers.

**Reflecting the Communion of the Trinity**

5. It is significant that in the priestly prayer at the Last Supper Jesus prayed not only for the consecration (of his Apostles) by means of truth,[12] but also for their unity, a unity reflecting the very communion of the divine Persons.[13] Although that prayer primarily concerned the Apostles whom Jesus wanted especially to gather around himself, it is extended also to bishops and presbyters, in addition to believers, of every age. Jesus asks that the priestly community be a reflection and participation in Trinitarian communion: what a sublime ideal!

Nevertheless, the circumstances in which Jesus offered his prayer show that sacrifices are required to achieve this ideal. Jesus asks for the unity of his Apostles and followers at the moment when he is offering his life to the Father. He established priestly communion in his Church at the price of his own sacrifice. Priests, therefore, cannot be surprised at the sacrifices that priestly communion requires of them. Taught by the word of Christ, they discover in these renunciations a concrete spiritual and ecclesial sharing in the divine Master's redeeming sacrifice.

## NOTES

1. Mt 16:24; Lk 9:23
2. Cf. *Lumen gentium*, n. 28; *Pastores dabo vobis*, n. 74
3. Cf. Lk 10:1; Mk 6:7
4. Mt 16:24
5. Eph 4:12, 16
6. Mk 3:14
7. Cf. Lk 22:28
8. Cf. Jn 15:4-11
9. Cf. Jn 13:2-15
10. Cf. Jn 13:34 15:12
11. Jn 17:21-23
12. Cf. Jn 17:17
13. Cf. Jn 17:11

# XV

# Priests: United to Bishops in Charity and Obedience

General Audience of Wednesday August 25, 1993

*The spirit of priestly communion demands that every priest exercise his ministry in respectful cooperation with the Bishop.*

1. The communion desired by Jesus between all who share in the sacrament of Orders should appear in an altogether special way in presbyters' relations with their bishops. On this subject the Second Vatican Council speaks of a "hierarchical communion" deriving from the unity of consecration and mission. We read: "All priests share with the bishops the one identical priesthood and ministry of Christ. Consequently the very unity of their consecration and mission requires their *hierarchical communion* with the order of Bishops. This unity is best shown on some occasions by liturgical concelebration, and priests also affirm their union with the bishops in the Eucharistic celebration."[1]

Clearly, the mystery of the Eucharist also appears here as a sign and source of unity. Connected with the Eucharist is the sacrament of Orders, which establishes the hierarchical communion between all those who share Christ's priesthood: "All priests then" the Council adds, "whether diocesan or religious, by reason of the sacrament of Orders and of the ministry correspond to and cooperate with the body of bishops."[2]

## Indispensable Coworkers of the Bishop

2. This bond between priests of any type or rank and the bishops is essential to exercising the priestly ministry. Priests receive from the Bishop sacramental power and hierarchical authorization for this ministry. Religious too receive this power and authorization from the bishop who ordains them priests and from the one who governs the diocese where they exercise their ministry.

Even when they belong to orders that are exempt from the jurisdiction of diocesan bishops in regard to their internal governance, they receive from the bishop, in accordance with the norm of canon law, the mandate and consent for their involvement and activity within the diocese. Exception must always be made of the authority by which the Roman Pontiff, as head of the Church, can confer on religious orders or other institutes the power to govern themselves according to their own constitutions and to work on a universal scale. In their turn bishops regard priests as "their indispensable helpers and advisers in the ministry and in the task of teaching, sanctifying and shepherding the People of God."[3]

3. Because of this bond of sacramental communion between priests and bishops, presbyters are a "support and instrument" of the episcopal order, as the Constitution *Lumen Gentium* states.[4] In each community they continue the bishop's action and in a certain way represent him as Pastor in various areas.

By virtue of its same pastoral identity and sacramental origin, the ministry of presbyters is clearly exercised "under the authority of the Bishop." According to *Lumen gentium*, it is under this authority that they lend "their efforts to the pastoral work of the whole diocese" by sanctifying and governing that portion of the Lord's flock entrusted to them.[5]

It is true that presbyters represent Christ and act in his name, sharing in his office as the one Mediator, according to their degree of ministry. However, they can act only as the bishop's coworkers, thus extending the ministry of the diocesan Pastor in the local communities.

4. Spiritually rich relationships between bishops and presbyters are based on this theological principle of sharing within the framework of hierarchical communion. *Lumen Gentium* describes these relationships as follows: "By reason of this sharing in the priesthood and mission of the bishop the priests should see in him a true father and obey him with all respect. The bishop, on his side, should treat the priests, his helpers, as his sons and friends, just as Christ calls his disciples no longer servants but friends."[6]

### Brothers and Friends of the Bishops

Here Christ's example is the rule of conduct for bishops and presbyters alike. If he who had divine authority did not want to treat his disciples as servants but as friends, the Bishop cannot consider his priests as servants in his employ. They serve the People of God with him. And for their part presbyters should respond to the Bishop as demanded by the law of reciprocal love in ecclesial and priestly communion: that is, as friends and spiritual "sons." The Bishop's authority and the obedience of his coworkers, the priests, should thus be exercised in an atmosphere of true, sincere friendship.

This duty is based not only on the brotherhood existing between all Christians by virtue of Baptism and on that arising from the sacrament of Orders, but also on the word and example of Jesus, who, even in triumph as the resurrected One, lowered himself from that incomparable height to his disciples and called them "my brothers", declaring that his Father was "theirs" too.[7]

Thus, following Jesus' example and teaching, the Bishop should treat his coworkers, the priests, as brothers and friends, without diminishing his authority as their Pastor and ecclesiastical superior. An atmosphere of brotherhood and friendship fosters the presbyters' trust and their willingness to cooperate and work harmoniously in friendship and in fraternal and filial charity toward their bishops.

5. The Council spells out some of the bishops' duties towards presbyters. Here one need only mention them: they should take the greatest interest they are capable of in the temporal and spiritual welfare of their priests; they should foster their sanctification and be concerned for their ongoing formation, examining with them problems that concern the needs of their pastoral work and the good of the diocese.[8]

Likewise, the presbyters' duties towards their bishops are summarized in these words: "Priests for their part should keep in mind the fullness of the sacrament of Orders which the bishops enjoy and should reverence in their persons the authority of Christ the supreme Pastor. They should therefore be attached to their Bishop with sincere charity and obedience."[9]

### Bearing Fruit in the Pastoral Ministry

Charity and obedience: two spiritual essentials which should guide their conduct towards their own Bishop. It is an *obedience* motivated by *charity*. The presbyter's basic intention in his ministry can only be to cooperate with his Bishop. If he has a spirit of faith, he recognizes the will of Christ in his Bishop's decisions.

Understandably, obedience can sometimes be more difficult, particularly when different opinions clash. However, obedience was Jesus' fundamental attitude in sacrificing himself and it bore fruit in the salvation that the whole world has received. The presbyter who lives by faith knows that he too is called to an obedience which, by fulfilling

Jesus' saying about self-denial, gives him the power and the glory of sharing the redemptive fruitfulness of the sacrifice of the cross.

6. Lastly it should be added that, as everyone knows today more than in the past, priests' cooperation and, thus, their union with the bishops are required by the pastoral ministry because of its complexity and vastness. As the Council says: "There is all the more need in our day for union of priests with bishops because in this age of ours apostolic enterprises must necessarily, for various reasons, take on many different forms. And not only that, but they must often overstep the bounds of one parish or diocese. Hence no priest is sufficiently equipped to carry out his own mission alone and as it were single-handed. He can only do so by joining forces with other priests, under the leadership of those who are rulers of the Church."[10]

For this reason "presbyteral councils" too have tried to structure and organize the consultation of priests by their bishops.[11] On their part, presbyters participate in these councils in a spirit of enlightened and loyal cooperation, with the intention of helping to build up the "one Body." Individually too, in their personal relations with their own Bishop they should remember and keep in mind one thing above all: the growth in charity of each and every one which is the fruit of self-sacrifice in the light of the cross.

## NOTES

1. *Presbyterorum ordinis*, n. 7
2. *Lumen gentium*, n. 28
3. *Presbyterorum ordinis*, n. 7
4. *Lumen gentium*, n. 28
5. *Ibid.*
6. *Ibid.*; cf. Jn 15:15
7. Cf. Jn 20:17, Mt 28:10
8. Cf. *Presbyterorum ordinis*, n. 7
9. *Ibid.*
10. *Ibid.*
11. Cf. 1971 Synod of Bishops: *Enchiridion Vaticanum*, IV, 1224

# XVI

# Priests: Charitable Cooperation among Brothers

General Audience of Wednesday September 1, 1993

*A brotherly spirit among priests should be reflected in a willingness to assist each other in a wide variety of ministries and apostolic works.*

1. The "priestly community" or presbyterate that we have spoken of in the preceding catecheses establishes among those who belong to it a network of reciprocal relationships that are situated within the ecclesial communion arising from Baptism. The most specific foundation of these relationships is the common sacramental and spiritual sharing in the priesthood of Christ, from which a spontaneous *sense of belonging* to the presbyterate stems.

The Council pointed this out clearly: "All priests, who are constituted in the order of the priesthood by the sacrament of Orders, are bound together by an intimate sacramental brotherhood; but in a special way they form one priestly body in the diocese to which they are attached under their own Bishop."[1] Because of mutual knowledge, closeness and habits of life and work, this relationship with the diocesan presbyterate further develops that *sense of belonging*, which creates and nurtures fraternal communion and opens it to pastoral cooperation.

The bonds of pastoral charity are expressed in the ministry and the liturgy, as the Council goes on to note: "Each is joined to the rest of the members of this priestly body by special ties of apostolic charity of ministry and of brotherhood. This is signified liturgically from ancient times by the fact that the priests present at an ordination are invited to impose hands, along with the ordaining bishop, on the chosen candidate, and when priests concelebrate the sacred Eucharist in a spirit of harmony."[2] In these cases there is a representation of sacramental communion, but also of that spiritual communion which in the liturgy finds the *una vox* to proclaim to God unity of spirit and to give testimony of it to the brothers and sisters.

### Regardless of Particular Duties: Fulfilling One's Priestly Service for the People

2. Priestly fraternity is also expressed in the unity of pastoral ministry, in the wide variety of tasks, offices and activities to which presbyters are assigned; "for even though they may be assigned different duties, yet they fulfill the one priestly service for people."[3]

The variety of duties can be considerable. Thus, for example: parish ministry and inter-parish and multi-parish ministry, diocesan, national and international activities, education, research, analysis, teaching in the various areas of religious and theological doctrine, every apostolate of giving witness, sometimes by studying and teaching various branches of human knowledge, spreading the Gospel message through the *media*, religious art in its many forms, the variety of charitable services, moral guidance to different categories o people involved in research or other work, and lastly, ecumenical activities, which are very timely and important today.

This variety cannot create classes or inequalities, because for priests these tasks always fall within the scope of evangelization. We say with the Council: "They all contribute to the same purpose, namely, the building up of the Body of Christ, and this, especially in our times demands many kinds of duties and fresh adaptations."[4]

3. Therefore, it is important for every priest to be willing— and properly trained—to understand and value the work performed by his brothers in the priesthood. It is a question of a Christian and ecclesial spirit, as well as an openness to the signs of the times. He will have to understand, for example, that there is a variety of needs in building up the Christian community, as there are a diversity of charisms and gifts; there is also a variety of ways to plan and carry out apostolic projects, since new work methods can be proposed and employed in the pastoral sphere, while always remaining within the Church's communion of faith and action.

Reciprocal understanding is the basis of mutual help in the various areas. Let us repeat what the Council said: "It is of great importance that all priests, whether diocesan or regular, should help each other, so that they may be fellow-helpers of the truth."[5] Reciprocal help can be given in many ways: from being willing to assist a confrère in need to accepting a work plan in a spirit of pastoral cooperation, which seems ever more necessary between the different agencies and groups and in the overall coordination of the apostolate.

In this regard, it should be kept in mind that the *parish* itself (as sometimes the *diocese* too), although having its autonomy, cannot be an island, especially at a time like our own, which abounds with means of communication, population mobility, the popularity of various attractions, a new uniformity of tendencies, attitudes, fashions, schedules. Parishes are the living organs of the one Body of Christ, the one Church, welcoming and serving both the members of the local communities and all those who for any reason come there at a given moment, which could mean that God has become visible in a conscience, in a life. Naturally, this should not become a source of disorder or confusion in regard to canon law, which is also at the service of pastoral care.

## Characterized by Kindness and Generosity

4. A particular effort of mutual understanding and reciprocal help is desirable and should be fostered especially in the relationships between older and younger priests: both are so necessary for the Christian community and so dear to bishops and to the Pope. The Council itself urged older priests to have understanding and sympathy for the projects of the younger ones, and advised the latter to have respect for the experience of their elders and to trust them; it recommended that both groups treat each other with sincere affection, in accordance with the example given by so many priests, past and present.[6]

How many things spring from the heart to the lips on these points, concretely showing the "priestly communion" that links presbyters! Let us be content to mention some things suggested by the Council: "Under the influence of a spirit of brotherhood, priests should not forget hospitality,[7] and should cultivate kindness and the sharing of goods.[8] They should be particularly concerned about those who are sick, about the afflicted, the overworked, the lonely, the exiled, the persecuted."[9]

When every pastor, every priest, looks back over his life he finds it strewn with experiences when he needed understanding, help, the cooperation of so many brothers as do other faithful, who find themselves with the various kinds of needs listed above; and with so many others! Who knows whether it would be possible to do more for all those *"poor"*, loved by the Lord and entrusted by him to the Church's charity, and also for those who, as the Council reminds us,[10] could be facing moments of crisis. Indeed, conscious of having followed the voice of the Lord and the Gospel, we must strive each day to do ever more and better for everyone.

5. The Council also suggests some community projects to foster mutual help in cases of need and in a permanent and almost institutional way on behalf of the brethren.

## Helping One Another Towards Holiness

First of all, it mentions periodic fraternal gatherings for rest and relaxation, in order to answer the human need for restoring one's physical, mental and spiritual strength, which Jesus, the "Teacher and Lord", in his careful attention to the condition of others, already had in mind when he invited the Apostles: "Come by yourselves to an out-of-the-way place and rest a little."[11] This invitation also applies to priests in every age, in ours more than ever, given the urgent tasks and their complexity in the pastoral ministry too.[12]

The Council thus encourages projects that are meant to provide and facilitate a common life for presbyters in a permanent way, including wisely established and organized arrangements for living together, or at least for an easily accessible and practical common table in appropriate places. The reasons for these provisions are not only economic and practical, but also spiritual and, in harmony with the institutions of the early Jerusalem community,[13] they are obvious and urgent in the modern condition of many presbyters and prelates, who must be offered attention and care to alleviate their difficulties and labors.[14]

"Associations of priests are also to be highly esteemed and diligently promoted, when by means of rules recognized by the competent authority they foster priestly holiness in the exercise of the ministry through a suitable and properly approved rule of life and through brotherly help, and so aim at serving the whole order of presbyters."[15]

6. In many places and in the past as well, holy priests have had this latter experience. The Council zealously desires that it be as widespread as possible; new institutions providing great benefit for the clergy and Christian people are

not wanting. Their growth and effectiveness vary in proportion to their fulfillment of the conditions laid down by the Council: the goal of priestly sanctification, fraternal help between priests, communion with ecclesiastical authority at the level of the diocese or the Apostolic See, according to the circumstances. This communion implies approved statutes as a rule of life and work, without which the members would almost inevitably be condemned to disorder or to the arbitrary impositions of some stronger personalities. It is an old problem for every type of association, and also occurs in the religious and ecclesiastical sphere.

The Church's authority fulfills its mission of service to priests and all the faithful also when it exercises this function of discerning authentic values, protecting people's spiritual freedom and guaranteeing the validity of associations as well as the whole life of the community.

Here too it is a question of realizing the holy ideal of "priestly communion."

# NOTES

1. *Presbyterorum ordinis,* n. 8
2. *Ibid.*
3. *Ibid.*
4. *Ibid.*
5. *Ibid.*
6. Cf. *ibid.*
7. Cf. Heb 13:1-2
8. Cf. Heb 13:16
9. Cf. Heb 13:16, cf. Mt 5:10
10. *Ibid.*
11. Mk 6:31
12. Cf. *Presbyterorum ordinis,* n. 8
13. Cf. Acts 2:46-47
14. Cf. *Presbyterorum ordinis,* n. 8
15. *Ibid.*

# XVII

# Priests: Servants of Christ's Flock

General Audience of Wednesday September 22, 1993

*Because the priest is set in the midst of lay people in order to lead them to unity, he must be a man of understanding and reconciliation.*

1. The "priestly community", of which we have spoken several times in previous catecheses, is not isolated from the "ecclesial community", but belongs to its very essence and is its very heart, in a constant interchange with all the other members of Christ's Body. Presbyters serve this vital communion as pastors in virtue of sacramental Orders and the mandate that the Church confers on them.

At the Second Vatican Council the Church sought to reawaken in priests this awareness of belonging and sharing, so that each of them would keep in mind that, although he is a pastor, he continues to be a Christian who must conform himself to all the demands of his Baptism and live as brother with all the baptized, in service to "the same Body of Christ which all are commanded to build up."[1]

It is significant that, on the basis of the ecclesiology of the Body of Christ, the Council stresses the fraternal nature of the priest's relations with the other faithful, as it had already underscored the fraternal nature of the bishop's rela-

tions with his presbyters. In the Christian community, relationships are essentially fraternal, as Jesus requested in
"his" commandment, recalled with such insistence by the
Apostle St. John in his Gospel and Letters.[2] Jesus himself
said to his disciples: "You are all brothers."[3]

### Supportive of the Lay Apostolate

2. According to Jesus' teaching, presiding over the community means serving it, not domineering over it. He himself
gave us the example of a Shepherd who cares for and serves
his flock, and he proclaimed that he came not to be served
but to serve.[4] In the light of Jesus, the Good Shepherd and
the one Teacher and Lord,[5] the priest understands that he
cannot seek his own honor nor his own interests, but only
what Jesus Christ wanted, putting himself at the service of
his kingdom in the world.

Thus, he knows—and the Council reminds him—that he
must act as the servant of all, with sincere and generous
self-giving, accepting all the sacrifices required by this service, and always remembering that Jesus Christ, the one
Teacher and Lord, came to serve and did so to the point of
giving "his own life as a ransom for the many."[6]

3. The problem of the presbyter's relationship with the other
faithful in the Christian community is particularly significant with regard to the so-called *lay apostolate*, which, as
such, has taken on special importance in our day because of
the new awareness of the essential role exercised by the lay
faithful in the Church.

Everyone knows that the same historical circumstances have
fostered the cultural and organizational rebirth of the lay
apostolate, especially in the 19th century, and how a theology of the lay apostolate developed in the Church between the two world wars, leading to the special conciliar
decree *Apostolicam actuositatem*, and even more fundamen-
tally, to the vision of the Church as community, which we
find in the Dogmatic Constitution *Lumen gentium*, and the
place for the lay apostolate it recognizes.

The Council considers priests' relationship with the laity in the light of the living, active and organic community which the priest is called to form and lead. To this end, the Council recommends that presbyters recognize and sincerely promote the *dignity* of the laity: their dignity as human persons raised by Baptism to divine adoption and endowed with their own gifts of grace.

For each of them, the divine gift entails a special role in the Church's mission of salvation, also in places—such as the family, civil society, professional life, culture, etc.—where presbyters ordinarily cannot exercise the laity's specific roles.[7]  Both the laity and priests must acquire an ever greater awareness of these specific roles, one based on a more complete sense of belonging to and participating in the Church.

4. The Council also says that presbyters should respect the just *freedom* of the laity, inasmuch as they are children of God enlivened by the Holy Spirit.  In this atmosphere of respect for dignity and freedom, the Council's exhortation to priests is understandable: "They should be willing to listen to lay people", taking into account their aspirations and utilizing their experience and competence in human activity, in order to recognize "the signs of the times".  Presbyters will also seek to discern, with the Lord's help, the laity's charisms, "whether humble or exalted", and will want to "recognize them with joy and foster them with diligence."[8]

What the Council notes and recommends is interesting and important: "Among the other gifts of God which are found abundantly among the faithful, special attention ought to be devoted to those graces by which a considerable number of people are attracted to greater heights of the spiritual life."[9]  Thanks be to God, we know that there are many faithful—in the Church today and often outside of her visible organizations—who are devoted or who want to devote themselves to prayer, meditation, penance (at least that of tiring, everyday work, done with diligence and patience, and that of difficult living situations), with or without the direct involvement in an active apostolate. They often feel the need for a priest counsellor or even a spiritual director, who welcomes them, listens to them and treats them with Christian friendship, in humility and charity.

### Encouraging the Laity regarding the Apostolate of the Church

One could say that the moral and social crisis of our time, with the problems it brings to both individuals and families, makes this need for priestly help in the spiritual life more keenly felt. A new recognition of and a new dedication to the ministry of the confessional and of spiritual direction are to be strongly recommended to priests, also because of the new requests of lay people who more greatly desire to follow the way of Christian perfection set forth by the Gospel.

5. The Council advises priests to recognize, promote and foster the cooperation of the laity in the apostolate and in the same pastoral ministry within the Christian community, not hesitating to "give lay people charge of duties in the service of the Church" and to "give them freedom and opportunity for activity and even inviting them, when opportunity occurs, to take initiative in undertaking projects on their own."[10]

This is consistent with respect for the dignity and freedom of the children of God, but also with Gospel service: "service to the Church", the Council says. It bears repeating that all this presupposes a deep sense of belonging to the community and of belonging to the community and of actively participating in its life. Even more deeply, it presumes faith and confidence in the grace at work in the community and in its members.

What the Council says could serve as a key to pastoral practice in this area, namely, that presbyters "have been placed in the midst of the laity that they may lead them all to the unity of charity."[11] Everything revolves around this central truth: in particular, openness and acceptance of everyone, the constant effort to maintain or restore harmony in order to encourage reconciliation, foster mutual understanding and create an atmosphere of peace. Yes, priests must always and everywhere be men of peace.

6. The Council entrusts this mission of community peace to priests: peace in truth and charity. "Theirs is the task, then, of bringing about agreement among divergent outlooks in such a way that nobody may feel a stranger in the Christian community. They are to be at once the defenders of the common good, for which they are responsible in the Bishop's name; and at the same time the unwavering champions of truth lest the faithful be carried about 'with every wind of doctrine'.[12] Those who have abandoned the practice of the sacraments, or even perhaps the faith, are entrusted to priests as special objects of their care. They will not neglect to approach these as good shepherds."[13]

Thus, they are concerned for everyone in and outside the flock, in accordance with the demands of the missionary dimension that pastoral work must have today. Against this background every presbyter will view the question of contacts with non-believers, the non-religious, even those who call themselves atheists. He will feel spurred by charity towards all; he will strive to open the doors of the community to everyone. On this point the Council calls priests' attention to "those fellow Christians who do not enjoy complete ecclesiastical union with us." This is the ecumenical horizon.

Finally, the Council invites them to "regard as committed to their charge all those who fail to recognize Christ as their Savior."[14] To make Christ known, to open the doors of minds and hearts to him, to cooperate with his ever new coming into the world: this the *raison d'être* of the pastoral ministry.

## Deserving of the Love and Support of the Laity

7. Through the Church priests have received a difficult charge from Christ.  It is quite understandable that the Council asks all the faithful to cooperate as far as they can, to help them in their work and their problems, first of all with understanding and love.  The faithful are the other element in the relationship of love linking priests to the whole community.  The Church, which urges priests to care for and to look after the community, calls the faithful  in turn to solidarity towards their pastors: "The faithful for their part ought to realize that they have obligations to their priests.  They should treat them with filial love as being their fathers and pastors.  They should also share their priests' anxieties and help them as far as possible by prayer and active work."[15]

The Pope says this again, addressing to all the lay faithful an urgent request in the name of Jesus, our one.Teacher and Lord: help your pastors by prayer and active work, love and support them in the daily exercise of their ministry.

## NOTES

1. *Presbyterorum ordinis*, n. 9
2. Cf.  Jn 13:14; 15:12, 17; 1 Jn 4:11, 21
3. Mt 23:8
4. Cf.  Mk 10:45; Mt 20:28
5. Cf.  Mt 23:8
6. Mt 20:28
7. Cf. *Presbyterorum ordinis*, n. 9
8. *Ibid.*
9. *Ibid.*
10. *Ibid.*
11. *Ibid.*
12. Eph 4:14
13. *Ibid.*
14. *Ibid.*
15. *Ibid.*

# XVIII

# Priests: Not Choosing God but Chosen by God

General Audience of Wednesday September 29, 1993

*Jesus Christ told his disciples to pray for vocations, and so everyone must work and pray that many young men will follow the Lord's call.*

"Non vos me elegistis sed ego elegi vos." It was not you who chose me, but I who chose you. With these words I would like to begin the catechesis which is part of the great cycle of catecheses on the Church. In this great cycle there is a catechesis on the vocation to the priesthood. The words Jesus spoke to the Apostles are symbolic and refer not only to the Twelve, but to all the generations of those whom Jesus Christ has called down the centuries. They refer to some in a personal way: we are speaking of the priestly vocation, but we are also thinking of the vocations of men and women to the consecrated life. It is a central problem for the Church, for the faith, for the future of the faith in this world: vocations.

Vocations, every vocation is a gift, a gift of God, according to these words of Jesus: I chose you. Thus it is a choice, an election by Jesus, one that always concerns the person. However, this person lives in the given context of a family, a society, a culture, a Church. Therefore, a vocation is a gift, but it is also the response to this gift. How each of us, how the one called, chosen, can answer this divine call depends on many circumstances. It depends on a certain inner, personal maturity; it depends on what is called cooperation with God's grace.

To know how to cooperate, how to listen, how to follow. We know well, we recall what Jesus said to that young man in the Gospel: "Follow me." To know how to follow: and when one follows, then the vocation is mature, the vocation is fulfilled, realized. And this is always for the good of the person and the community.

The community, for its part, must know how to respond to these vocations that arise within it. They are born in the family and the family must be able to cooperate with a vocation. They are born in the parish, and the parish must be able to cooperate with a vocation. These are the circumstances of human life, of human existence: existential circumstances.

A vocation, the response to a vocation, depends to a very high degree on the witness of the whole community, the family, the parish. It is people who help vocations to grow. It is priests who by their example attract young men and help them respond to Jesus' words: "Follow me." Those who have received a vocation must be able to give an example of how to follow.

In the parish today it is increasingly apparent that movements and associations are contributing in a special way to the growth of vocations and to vocation work. One of the movements or associations that is typical of the parish is that of the altar boys, the servers.

This fact is a great help to future vocations, as it was in the past. Many who first were altar boys, later became priests. It is still useful today, but other ways must be tried. Other methods we could say: how to cooperate with the divine call, with the divine choice; how to fulfil, or help to fulfil these words of Jesus: the harvest is great, but the workers are few. This is true. The harvest is always great; the workers are always few, especially in some countries.

However, Jesus says: pray for this to the Lord of the harvest. For us all, therefore, without exception, there remains above all the pain of praying for vocations. If we feel involved in the redeeming work of Christ and the Church, we must always pray for vocations. The harvest is great.

Praised be Jesus Christ!

# XIX

# Priests: Discovering Priestly Identity in the Eucharist

Audience with prelates attending the plenary assembly
of the Congregation for the Clergy, October 22, 1993

*Priesthood is a gift from heaven which we must correspond-
ingly welcome with gratitude, loving it and giving it to others.*

Your Eminences,

Venerable Brothers in the Episcopate and in the Priesthood,

1. I am particularly pleased to welcome you today, together
with the members, experts and officials of the Congregation for the Clergy, gathered in plenary session.

I am grateful to the Prefect of the dicastery, Cardinal José
Sánchez, for his words of introduction to the reflections
made during these days, and I also thank the Secretary,
Archbishop Crescenzio Sepe, for his valuable assistance.

I would like, above all, to express my grateful satisfaction
for the work you have done, work which has involved the
whole Episcopate in matters of the utmost importance. At
the same time I encourage you all so that, as soon as possible, the bishops, and through them all priests, may be

provided with a Directory for the life, ministry and permanent formation of priests. This, as you know well, has been requested by many prelates throughout the world, as well as by the 1990 Ordinary Assembly of the Synod of Bishops and by numerous priests in the care of souls.

## Acting in the Person of Christ the Head

It is more than ever urgent, in this age of ours marked by a widespread, although sometimes unexpressed thirst for values, that the ministers of the altar, ever spiritually aware of their great vocation, should be formed to carry out their pastoral and missionary ministry with fidelity and competence.

2. "Before I formed you in the womb", says the Lord to the prophet Jeremiah, "I knew you, before you were born I dedicated you, a prophet to the nations I appointed you."[1]

For an authentic priestly life it is absolutely necessary to have a clear awareness of one's own vocation! The priesthood is a gift which comes from God in the image of the vocation of Christ, the High Priest of the new covenant: "No one takes this honour upon himself but only when called by God, just as Aaron was."[2]  Indeed, it is not a question of "function", but rather of God's free and exclusive "vocation" to which, as he calls man into being, calls him also to the priesthood, not without the mediation of the Church. With the laying on of hands by the bishop and the prayer of consecration, he is made a minister who continues the work of salvation accomplished by God through Christ in the Holy Spirit.

"The priesthood of priests", the Second Vatican Council reminds us, "while presupposing the sacraments of initiation is nevertheless conferred by its own particular sacrament. Through that sacrament priests, by the anointing of the Holy Spirit, are signed with a special character and so are configured to Christ the Priest in such a way that they are able to act in the person of Christ the Head."[3]

Acting *"in persona Christi Capitis"*,[4] the priest proclaims the divine Word, celebrates the Eucharist and dispenses the merciful love of God who forgives; in this way he becomes an instrument of life, renewal and authentic human progress.

As minister of the essential saving acts, he places at the service of all men not perishable goods, nor socio-political projects, but supernatural and eternal life, teaching how to read and interpret the events of history in a Gospel perspective.

This is the primary task of the priest, even in the area of the new evangelization, which requires priests who, as primarily responsible together with their Bishops for this renewed Gospel sowing, are "deeply and fully immersed in the mystery of Christ."[5]

3. The priesthood of the sacred ministers shares in the unique priesthood of Christ, made Priest and Intercessor through the offering of his own sacrifice, offered once and for all on the cross.[6]

In order to have an adequate understanding of the ordained priesthood, and to deal correctly with every question concerning the identity, life, service and ongoing formation of priests, it is necessary to be always aware of the sacrificial nature of the Eucharist, of which they are the ministers.

Priestly identity shines forth in a very special way in the Eucharist. Assimilation to Christ hinges on it, it is the basis of an ordered life of prayer and genuine pastoral charity.

4.   Configured to the Redeemer, the Head and Shepherd of the Church the priest must be clearly aware that he is, in a new way, Christ's minister for his people.[7]

An "awareness of being a pastoral minister" is proper only to the one who is "sent", in imitation of the Good Shepherd, to be the leader and shepherd of the flock, in joyful and complete self-giving to all his brothers and sisters, especially those who are in most need of love and mercy.

5. In imitation of the divine Master, the priest is called to make *a gift of his own will* and to become an extension as it were of *Christus oboediens* for the salvation of the world.

## Sons, Brothers and Friends of the Bishop

The example of Christ is a light and strength for bishops and priests. The Bishop, for his part, by his obedience to the Apostolic See and communion with the whole body of bishops, creates the most favourable conditions for establishing a similar relationship with the presbyterate and each of its members.

Modelled on the relationship between Jesus and his disciples, *the bishop* must treat his priests as sons, brothers and friends, being concerned above all for their sanctification, but also for their physical well-being, their peace of mind, their proper rest, and assistance in all stages and conditions of life. All this not only does not diminish, but better illustrates his pastoral authority which, in a spirit of genuine service, is able to assume those responsibilities of leadership which are personal, cannot be delegated and are sometimes even arduous and complex.

Such example nurtures the trust of the priests and stimulates their desire for regular cooperation and sincere brotherhood. What a precious gift is *priestly brotherhood!* It is a comfort in difficulties, solitude, misunderstanding and weariness, and is conducive, by the example of the first apostolic community, to concord and peace, "to proclaim to God unity of spirit and to give witness of it to the brothers and sisters."[8]

6. In this climate of active priestly communion, the *ongoing formation* of priests will also find the best conditions for development and for bearing abundant fruit; therefore it is necessary to train well-qualified and faithful ministers.

In the work of formation the authoritative and at the same time brotherly care of the Bishop for his priests, and on their part the awareness of the constant need to deepen the great gift of their vocation and the responsibility of their ministerial commitment intertwine in a positive way.

This is a theme which has been at the heart of your considerations in this plenary assembly, and one which will find an adequate response in the "Directory" you are preparing.

7. In reality, every plan for priestly formation must have as its principal aim the *sanctification of the clergy*. Indeed, if it is true that the word and the sacraments work through the power of the Spirit they impart, it is also true that, when they transform the life of the minister, he himself becomes a kind of living Gospel. The best evangelizer is always a holy one.

In a special way, *prayer* is necessary for the priest to sanctify himself and the souls entrusted to him.

The underlying principle, the virtue which shapes and guides his spiritual life, is the *pastoral charity* flowing from the merciful heart of Jesus the Savior. The essential meaning of this pastoral charity is the radical gift of self to the Church which, as a consequence, is the primary interest of the well-formed and mature priest. Priestly life is, in effect, an aspect of the wonderful mystery of the Mystical Body, and therefore cannot be interpreted correctly by purely human criteria.

For example, the more the Church, led by the Spirit, enters into the truth of Christ's priesthood, the more she is joyfully aware of the gift of *sacred celibacy* (which is seen less and less as a matter of discipline, however noble), so as to be open to the horizon of its singular appropriateness for the sacrament of Holy Orders.[9]

Ecclesiastical celibacy is for the Church a treasure to be carefully guarded and to be presented especially today as a sign of contradiction for a society which needs to be called back to the higher and definitive values of life.

Present difficulties cannot cause the rejection of such a precious gift, which the Church has made her own uninterruptedly from apostolic times, overcoming other difficult moments that threatened its preservation. It is necessary today, too, to interpret concrete situations with faith and humility, without introducing anthropological, sociological or psychological factors that, while seeming to resolve problems, actually add to them beyond measure.

Gospel logic, as the facts prove, demonstrates clearly that the noblest aims are always hard to achieve. We must work hard, then, and never turn back! So it is always most important to take the road of a courageous and incisive vocation's apostolate, in the sure knowledge that the Lord will not fail to provide labourers for his harvest if young people are offered high ideals and visible examples of austerity, consistency, generosity and unconditional dedication.

### Gifts of God for the Whole Church

Truly, the priesthood is a gift from on high, which we must correspondingly welcome with gratitude, loving it and giving it to others. It is not to be considered as a purely human reality, as if it were the expression of a community which democratically elects its Pastor. Rather, it is to be seen in the light of the *sovereign will of God who freely chooses his Pastors.* Christ wanted his Church to be sacramentally and hierarchically structured, and for this reason no one has the right to change what the divine Founder has established.

8. The Eternal High Priest, on the cross, gave John as a son to his Blessed Mother, and to John he entrusted his Mother as a precious inheritance. From that day there has been established a unique spiritual bond between Mary most holy and every priest. Because of this bond, Mary can obtain and give to her beloved sons the strength to respond ever more generously to the demands of spiritual sacrifice that accompany the priestly ministry.[10]

Beloved brothers, let us entrust the priests of the whole world to her, the Queen of Apostles; let us entrust to her maternal heart those who are preparing to become priests; let us place confidently in her hands our humble but sincere intentions to commit ourselves in every way to their good.

May all priests feel moved to consecrate themselves to the Immaculate Virgin: they will certainly experience peace joy and pastoral fruitfulness from being her sons!

This is my wish, which becomes my prayer. A special Apostolic Blessing goes with it, which I gladly impart to all of you present and to the priests working in all parts of the world.

## NOTES

1. Jer 1:5
2. Heb 5:4
3. *Presbyterorum ordinis*, n. 2
4. *Ibid.*, also nn. 6, 12; *Sacrosanctum Concilium* n. 33, *Lumen gentium*, nn. 10, 28, 37
5. *Pastores dabo vobis*, n. 18
6. Cf. Heb 7:27
7. *Pastores dabo vobis*, n. 21
8. John Paul II, Catechesis, in *L'Osservatore Romano*, n. 36, Sep. 8, 1993, p. 11
9. Cf. *Pastores dabo vobis*, n. 50
10. Cf. John Paul II, General Audience, in *L'Osservatore Romano*, n. 27, July 7, 1993, p. 11

# XX

# Priests: During Mass, Aware of an Infinitely Surpassing Gift

Homily on November 1, 1993

Dear Brothers and Sisters,

1. Today, as every year, we celebrate the Eucharistic sacrifice here, in the ancient Roman cemetery of Verano. We celebrate it on the vigil of the Commemoration of our dear departed, as we contemplate the mystery of holiness on the Solemnity of All Saints.

This is a great day for the pilgrim Church on earth, a day of special closeness to those who have preceded us on this earth and are now standing "before the Lamb".[1] Their hearts are full of God's glory. This is the glorious day of "All Saints" which commemorates *the salvation brought to fulfillment in human history by the blood of the Redeemer.*

"A great multitude . . . from every nation, race, people and tongue. . . . 'Who are these . . . and where did they come from?'. . . 'These are the ones who have survived the time of great distress; they have washed their robes and made them white in the blood of the Lamb.'"[2]

The day of All Saints—the day of redemption fulfilled, the great feast of the Lamb of God, who takes away the sins of the world.

2. This day is imprinted indelibly in my memory. It was in fact on the Solemnity of All Saints 47 years ago that *I received the gift of Christ's priesthood and became a servant of the Eucharist.* I remember with constant devotion those who accompanied me on the way to this ministry. With them I unite myself in the mystery of the Communion of Saints.

On these days, the first and second of November, I was able to complete the journey which leads a new priest to the celebration of his first holy Mass: from the celebration with my Bishop (Cardinal Adam Stefan Sapieha) during the priestly ordination, *to the first Mass we could call "my own."* However, a Mass can never be said to be one's own! The Mass is always the sacrifice of Christ and of the whole Church, his Mystical Body. Holy Mass thus represents a profound entering into the mystery of All Saints, as indeed it is a meeting with those who, suffering in purgatory, "seek the face of God."[3]

### Never Forgetting the First Mass

Every holy Mass announces what is proclaimed in today's liturgy in the responsorial psalm: *"The Lord's are the earth and its fullness, the world and those who dwell in it."*[4] Yes! The redeeming sacrifice of Christ embraces everything and everyone. Aware of his own limitations, the priest celebrating Mass always experiences a gift which surpasses him infinitely.

3. *On the morning of the day of the Commemoration of All the Faithful Departed, I was able to celebrate the Eucharist* together with those who "seek the face of God",[5] united with them all. As the liturgy emphasizes, they see him "as he is".[6]

My mind's eye still sees the place, the crypt below the cathedral of Wawel, in Kraków, where the mortal remains of
the kings, great leaders and prophetic spiritual leaders of
my country lie. Their presence and their witness permeate
the cathedral, just as one notes in St. Peter's Basilica the
spiritual power radiating in a significant way from the
tombs of the Popes. *These are witnesses of history* in which
all nations, from generation to generation, together with
the Church seek "the face of the God of Jacob",[7] because, as
St. Augustine recalls, the heart of man is restless until it
rests in God.[8]

4. *That day, the day of one's first Mass, one never forgets.* It
remains not only in the memory, but is perpetuated in the
Eucharist of Christ, which is the same, yesterday, today and
forever. It is prolonged in the priestly ministry, as the
foundation of the vocation of every bishop, and especially
the Bishop of Rome.

*Celebrating the Eucharistic sacrifice here in Campo Verano,* I
would like to include in our common prayer all the cem-
eteries of Rome, and also those who "dwell" there. Not
only the dead of this city which is called "eternal", but "the
world, and those who dwell in it":[9] everyone, wherever
their mortal remains may lie, wherever they may be buried,
sometimes even without the proper respect their bodies
deserve (and sadly places of this kind are none too few . . .).

The redeeming sacrifice of Christ *embraces them all.* They
are present in this sacrifice of the Church, which prays on
behalf of the dead. The complete sacrifice of Christ, and at
the same time, the complete sacrifice for all men: for the
living and the dead.

5. "Who are these . . . and where did they come from?"[10]
From everywhere. From everywhere . . . "My Lord, you are
the one who knows."[11] From wherever they come they have
all "washed their robes and made them white with the
blood of the Lamb."[12] And now they are standing before
you.

Lord! May they see the face of the Father.  May they see you, the living God. May they see God, as he is.

Amen!

## NOTES

1. Cf.  Rv 7:9
2. Cf.  Rv 7:9, 13-14
3. Cf.  Ps 24
4. Ps 24:1
5. Cf.  Ps 24:6
6. I Jn 3:2
7. Cf.  Ps 24:6
8. Cf. *Confessions* 1:1
9. Ps 24:1
10. Rv 7:13
11. Rv 7:14
12. Rv 7:14

# XXI

# Priests: Granted the Gift of Celibacy through Humble Prayer

Address to the Bishops of Eastern Canada at the conclusion of their *ad limina* visits on November 8, 1993

*There is an essential link between the nature of the Eucharist and the ordained priesthood; and there is also a profound connection between the ordained priesthood and celibacy.*

Dear Brother bishops,

1. With great joy I welcome you—the *bishops of New Brunswick, Newfoundland, Nova Scotia and Prince Edward Island:* "Grace to you and peace from him who is and who was and who is to come."[1] Our meeting manifests the *profound spiritual and visible communion which exists between your particular churches and the Church universal,* a communion which springs from our being "grafted" into Christ.[2] We must constantly turn to him, the chief Shepherd,[3] in order to realize what are the "unsearchable riches"[4] with which he has invested us for the building up of the spotless spouse.[5] She it is whom he unites to himself by an unbreakable covenant, and whom he unceasingly "nourishes and cherishes".[6] Our unfailing trust and confidence rests in him and in the power of his Gospel to save.[7]

Following upon the *ad limina* visits of your brother bishops from Quebec and from the West and North, your presence is a reminder of the vastness of your land which extends *a mari usque ad mare*[8] and which presents so many challenges for the "new evangelization." With the other bishops I reflected on some aspects of their pastoral care of the Church and I encouraged them to be vigilant guardians of the truth, shepherds who proclaim the full truth of Christ and the Church. Today our thoughts turn to some other aspects of your ministry.

2. *As pastors you are called to feed your flocks,* refreshing their souls[9] with the abundant life won by the Good Shepherd as he freely gave himself up to death on the cross.[10] At the center of your sacramental ministry is the Eucharistic sacrifice, offered to nourish the faithful with the Bread which gives life to the world.[11] In some cases the *shortage or uneven distribution of priests* makes it difficult to meet the faithful's need for the Eucharist—the very source centre and culmination of the Church's life.[12] This situation, coupled with a critical decline in the number of Catholics attending Sunday Mass, calls for *vigorous pastoral action that is faithful to Church teaching.*

### Absolutely Necessary for the Existence of the Church

In meeting this challenge, certain fundamental principles should always guide your pastoral response. The parish is a community of the baptized who express and confirm their identity through the celebration of the Eucharistic sacrifice.[13] *This requires the presence of an ordained priest* whose first privilege and irreplaceable responsibility is to offer the Eucharist *in persona Christi.*[14] *Great care must be taken to ensure that no misunderstanding arises about the nature of the Eucharist and its essential link with the ordained priesthood.*

When a community is deprived of the priest who acts publicly in the name of Christ,[15] this regretable situation calls for an emergency response. Sunday celebrations should continue, and the lay persons who lead their brothers and sisters in prayer are exercising in a commendable way the common priesthood of all the faithful, based on the grace of Baptism. It would be a serious mistake, however, to accept this as a normal way of involving religious and lay men and women in the liturgy. *Such provisions should be regarded as only temporary, while the community is "in expectation of a priest".*[16] Your assiduous oversight is required so that all will see "the substitutional character of these celebrations, which should not be regarded as the optimal solution to new difficulties."[17]

Your Pastoral Letter *The Ministry of Priests* (18 January 1990) reaffirmed the Church's tradition when it stated unequivocally that "a Church without priests is unthinkable." On the contrary, the sacramental incompleteness of these celebrations should lead the whole community to pray more fervently that the Lord send labourers into his harvest.[18] And I join you in pleading with him that the Church in Canada may experience a fresh springtime of priestly and religious vocations.

3. The forthcoming apostolic visitations of your seminaries will provide the Episcopal Conference of Canada with ample opportunity to reflect on ways of *improving the human, spiritual, intellectual and pastoral formation of priests.* In the light of the relevant documents of the Holy See and the Post-Synodal Apostolic Exhortation *Pastores dabo vobis,* the updated *ratio fundamentalis* which you intend to draw up[19] will address the challenging task of deepening—both among the faithful and the candidates themselves—an understanding of *the ontological bond uniting the priest to Christ,* the High Priest and Good Shepherd. In this way the whole community will have a correct awareness and esteem for the priest's transcendent mission of being "the means and the living instrument for conferring God's grace" upon his people.[20]

## Celibacy and Configuration to Christ

4. At this time, when some question the desirability of maintaining the discipline of priestly celibacy, *bishops must courageously teach the fittingness of linking this "sign of contradiction" with the ministerial priesthood.* On the basis of her experience and reflection, the Church has discerned, with growing clarity through the ages, that priestly celibacy is not just a legal requirement imposed as a condition for ordination. It is profoundly connected with a man's configuration to Christ, the Good Shepherd and Spouse of the Church. As *Pastores dabo vobis* states: "Certainly it is a grace which does not dispense, with but counts most definitely on, a conscious and free response on the part of the receiver. This charism of the Spirit also brings with it the grace for the receiver to remain faithful to it for all his life and be able to carry out generously and joyfully its concomitant commitments."[21]

Cultural considerations, and the scarcity of priests in certain regions, sometimes give rise to calls for a change in this discipline. *To give decisive weight to solutions based on criteria deriving more from certain currents of anthropology, sociology or psychology than from the Church's living tradition* is certainly not the path to follow. We cannot overlook the fact that the Church comes to know the divine will *through the interior guidance of the Spirit,*[22] and that the difficulties involved today in keeping celibacy are not sufficient reason to overturn the Church's conviction regarding its value and appropriateness, a conviction constantly reaffirmed by the Church's Magisterium, not least by the Second Vatican Council.[23] Like the Church in other countries, the Church in Canada is called to face this situation *with* faith and courage, trusting "in the Spirit that the gift of celibacy . . . will be generously bestowed by the Father, as long as those who share in Christ's priesthood through the sacrament of Orders, and indeed the whole Church, humbly and earnestly pray for it."[24]

The scandal given by those members of the clergy and those religious who have failed in this regard has been a source of great suffering for the Church in Canada. I wish you to know that *I have personally shared this anguish with you* and that it has been the cause of much prayer to the "Father of mercies and God of all comfort"[25] for those who have been victims of sexual misconduct, as well as for those who have been guilty of it. Let us abide by Saint Paul's sound counsel: "Do not be overcome by evil but overcome evil with good."[26] Recalling with profound gratitude the fidelity and zeal of so many priests in Canada who, with pure and selfless hearts, have made the total gift of themselves to Christ and his Church, I ask you to convey my encouragement to every priest whose father in God you are.[27]

### Addressing the Rights of Women

5. Among your pastoral concerns, you are also called upon to address the vital question of the role of women, with their rights and duties, in your particular Churches and in Canadian society. The whole People of God needs to recognize and rejoice in *the irreplaceable gifts of "feminine genius" that women bring to the life and mission of the Church.*[28] These rich gifts of femininity originate with the first covenant of creation, which confers on woman "an expression of the 'image and likeness of God' that is specifically hers."[29] In the new covenant, which seals the redemptive union of Christ and the Church,[30] women enjoy a special priority in the "order of love".[31]

Since "God entrusts the human being to her in a special way",[32] woman's commitment to the home, marriage and family should not be seen as restrictive or demeaning. Rather that commitment reflects, in a profound and specific, though not exclusive way, the love which God himself has for his creation insofar as he cares personally for every one of his sons and daughters.[33] In this perspective it constitutes a serious pastoral responsibility, as well as a matter of charity and justice, to foster the authentic advancement of women, *which will be achieved only if it is anchored in the truth of creation and of divine Revelation.*

6. In the time remaining before the celebration of the 1994 Synod on "Consecrated Life and its Role in the Church and the World", I wish to call on the men and women religious of Canada to prepare for this event by ever more fervent prayer and reflection. *Religious life is a gift of the Spirit "to" the Church and "for" the Church.* Your extensive system of Catholic schools and hospitals would never have been established and could not continue its mission without the vision, determination and self-sacrifice of thousands of religious.  I think especially of the heroic labours of St. Marguerite Bourgeoys, St. Marguerite d'Youville—Canada's first native born saints—and Bl. Marie Léonie Paradis at whose beatification I presided during my Pastoral Visit to your country.

Yet you are all sadly aware that among certain groups the ideal of the religious life has lost ground in recent years, and we must hope that Canadian religious will use the occasion of the Synod "to reconsider the subject of their own renewal in light of the challenges and the opportunities of the present moment."[34] *It is especially urgent that they meditate on their common identity and foundational charism.*  In a spirit of profound humility and trusting in the power of him who "is able to do far more abundantly than all that we ask or think",[35] religious should examine to what extent the renewal envisaged by the Second Vatican Council has in fact taken place,[36] and borne the expected fruits of holiness and apostolic zeal. As shepherds of the whole community in your dioceses, your own ministry extends to the religious present in your local churches.  They need your support and guidance not just in their pastoral activities but also in promoting the observance of the evangelical counsels, whereby they are "consecrated to God in Jesus Christ as his exclusive possession."[37]

7. Dear brother bishops, it is towards evening of the second millennium, whose days are now far spent.[38] I appeal to you, as pastors of the Church in Canada, to begin preparations for the great Jubilee of our Lord's redemptive incarnation. Above all, *strengthen and encourage, in every phase of pastoral life, a new "ardor for holiness"*[39] among priests, religious and laity. As Shepherds after the Lord's own heart,[40] lead the Catholic faithful to the wellspring of life: "and this is eternal life, that they may know you, the only true God, and Jesus Christ whom you have sent."[41]

Relying upon the intercession of the saints of Canada, and entrusting you and all those in your pastoral care to the loving protection of our Lady, I cordially impart my Apostolic Blessing.

# NOTES

1. Rv 1:4
2. Cf. Rom 11:17 ff.
3. Cf. 1 Pt 5:4
4. Eph 3:8
5. Cf. Rv 19:7
6. Eph 5:29; Cf. *Lumen gentium*, n. 6
7. Cf. Rom 1:16
8. Cf. Ps 72:8
9. Cf. Ps 23:3
10. Cf. Jn 10:10-11
11. Cf. Jn 6:51
12. Cf. *Lumen gentium*, n. 11
13. Cf. *Christifideles laici*, n. 26
14. Cf. *Lumen gentium*, n. 10; *Pastores dabo vobis*, n. 48
15. Cf. *Presbyterorum ordinis*, n. 2
16. Congregation for Divine Worship, *Directory for Sunday Celebrations*, 2 June 1988, n. 27
17. *Ibid.*, n. 21
18. Cf. Mt 9:38
19. Cf. *From Pain to Hope*, VII, Recommendation 50

# Index